THE ULTIMATE GUIDE TO SMART PARENTING: 2 IN 1 BUNDLE

ALUE EDITION BOX SET FOR POSITIVE PARENTING TECHNIQUES TO REDUCE STRESS AND RAISE HAPPIER, SMARTER KIDS.

SIENNA NEEL

© **Copyright 2020 - All rights reserved.**

The content contained within this book may not be reproduced, duplicated or transmitted without direct written permission from the author or the publisher.

Under no circumstances will any blame or legal responsibility be held against the publisher, or author, for any damages, reparation, or monetary loss due to the information contained within this book, either directly or indirectly.

Legal Notice:

This book is copyright protected. It is only for personal use. You cannot amend, distribute, sell, use, quote or paraphrase any part, or the content within this book, without the consent of the author or publisher.

Disclaimer Notice:

Please note the information contained within this document is for educational and entertainment purposes only. All effort has been executed to present accurate, up to date, reliable, complete information. No warranties of any kind are declared or implied. Readers acknowledge that the author is not engaged in the rendering of legal, financial, medical or professional advice. The content within this book has been derived from various sources. Please consult a licensed professional before attempting any techniques outlined in this book.

By reading this document, the reader agrees that under no circumstances is the author responsible for any losses, direct or indirect, that are incurred as a result of the use of the information contained within this document, including, but not limited to, errors, omissions, or inaccuracies.

CONTENTS

SHHHH...LISTEN!

Introduction	11
1. Why Understanding Child Psychology is Important	17
2. Become the Master of Your Emotions	32
3. The Missing Step in Most Parenting Relationships	58
4. So How Do You Get Your Child to Listen to You?	80
5. Start Doing This and Watch What Happens in 7 Days!	98
6. The One Vital Skill Your Kids Might Be Struggling With and How to Fix It!	128
7. Now Let's Make Learning Fun!	146
Conclusion	157
References	161

RAISING EMOTIONAL INTELLIGENCE IN KIDS

Introduction	167
1. What Is Emotional Intelligence?	173
2. Cracking the Emotion Coach Code	195
3. Do You Need Emotional Intelligence In The Curriculum?	217
4. Coping with Aggressive or Defiant Kids the Smart Way	240
5. The Ultimate Guide To Mindfulness	272

6. What Every Parent Ought To Know About   290
   Dealing with Difficult Situations
7. The Ninja Guide To Build Resilience in Your   304
   Child
   Conclusion   325
   References   329

SHHHH...LISTEN!

PRACTICAL PARENTING STEPS TO GET YOUR KIDS TO LISTEN THAT WORK! AGE 3-8

This book is dedicated to my Mother

Who divided her love amongst six children and each child still had all her love

Ram.P

My Top 7 Essential Games to Boost Communication Skills In Children

(Make Learning Fun WIth These Perfect Tools !)

Checklist Includes:

- 7 Essential Games to Aid Child Development.
- Improve Family Bonding
- Encourages creativity and boost's self confidence
- Links to where you an buy these games for lowest prices.

If your're looking for hacks to accelerate your childs development then this is for you ....

   Visit the Link Or Scan the QR Code to get this FREE Bonus Checklist

https://tinyurl.com/Sienna-Checklist

INTRODUCTION

"Raising children is a creative endeavor, an art rather than a science."

— BRUNO BETTELHEIM

We've all heard that classic parental phrase for when we want to get our kids to do something: "Because I said so." Maybe we've even used it ourselves a few times. After all, we're the parents, so we rely on that level of authority. But if you think back to when you were a kid, you'll probably remember that "because I said so" wasn't exactly the most compelling argument. Instead of following along with a parent's advice, kids who hear it are more likely to resist the advice, all because of the poor communication inherent in the phrase.

Whether you're a new parent feeling out of your comfort zone, someone who wants to have a less volatile relationship between yourself and your child, or an educator who's having trouble getting some of the kids in your class to behave, improving your communication skills for talking with kids can significantly improve kids' behavioral issues and your relationship with them.

You know how difficult it can be to get your child to listen to you sometimes. They might be perfect angels one day, saying "please" and "thank you" and cleaning up after playtime, and the next they seem like completely different people, stubborn and prone to tantrums. You want what's best for your child, and you understand things about the world that they might not yet know themselves, so you try to guide them in the right direction. However, when you are unable to properly communicate with your child, this advice can lead to an argument and frequently ends in tears—possibly for both of you. The whole ordeal can leave you feeling uncertain about the relationship between yourself and your child, and even questioning your parenting skills.

The good news is that any adult can learn how to improve their communication with kids. With better knowledge of child psychology and the importance of clear communication, you can talk to your child in a way that helps them understand their own feelings and your wishes and goals for them. In this book, you'll learn about the way your child thinks, how kids process emotions, and what you can do to speak to them in a way they'll understand. You'll also learn strategies for fostering better communication skills for both yourself and your child.

Child development can be intimidating. You might worry that your child isn't getting the tools they need to grow and learn properly, especially if there is trouble communicating. But with a little help, you can ensure your child is well on his or her way to a healthy, happy life.

Child development includes multiple milestones that kids reach at their own pace. In the phase of early childhood, which lasts from birth to about eight years old, your child goes through the most development in the shortest amount of time. They learn to walk and talk—and that means communication skills. As your child begins school and forms friendships with classmates, they'll learn more about the world around them. Communication skills become very important during this period, as your child will want to ask questions and form bonds with others. Practicing good communication at home can significantly improve their ability to communicate with peers and teachers in an honest and clear way.

I am a personal life coach who has been working with kids for more than 10 years. I have helped many parents learn the principles for communicating effectively with their kids—and have helped just as many kids develop the communication skills they'll need for the rest of their lives. In my studies of child behavioral psychology, I have learned and instilled the socialization methods necessary to encourage healthy child development. With this book, I hope to help you understand and practice these methods in order to improve your relationship with your child, and your child to listen.

Establishing healthy communication with your child can significantly improve the parent-child relationship. When disagreements arise, they will no longer be the source of anger and tears; instead, they will be opportunities for your child to learn and for you to guide them through the often-confusing world around them. Your child will listen to you not because they feel they have to, but because they understand why you're telling them they can or can't do something. This creates a healthier bond between the two of you, one based on trust and honesty.

By improving your communication skills and those of your child, you ensure your child is receiving the developmental guidance they need as they grow up. As they move on to middle childhood and adolescence, they will be equipped with the tools they need to understand and convey their emotions to their peers. Healthy communication skills early on in life allow them to continue to thrive and maintain a positive relationship with you for years to come.

1

WHY UNDERSTANDING CHILD PSYCHOLOGY IS IMPORTANT

We often think of kids as just smaller versions of ourselves. We might assume they think the same way we do, but in actuality this is far from the truth. Kids are still developing, so their minds work very differently from our own. They haven't experienced all of the socialization and growth that we have, so they can have trouble grasping certain concepts or worldviews. Kids also take in and process information differently than we do. This causes a lot of frustration when it comes to getting kids to listen.

Often, the problem isn't a purposefully stubborn or disobedient child. Instead, the root of the issue is that we don't account for how a child processes what we tell them. Recognizing that child psychology is separate from adult psychology is the first step in addressing communication issues.

The idea that kids think differently than we do wasn't extensively embraced until the early 1930s. The person most responsible for changing how we think about childhood development was the Swiss psychologist Jean Piaget, who theorized that kids actually experience the world differently than adults. When he heard this theory, Albert Einstein reportedly said the discovery was "so simple that only a genius could have thought of it" (Cherry, 2019, para. 2). It might not be something we assume immediately, but when we start thinking of kids in this new light, many of their behaviors start to make a lot more sense. This is the basis of child psychology.

By accounting for developmental differences, we can forge a closer bond with our kids because we're able to meet them on their level. We can explain things in ways that make sense to them, and in turn can find it easier to understand their perspective. For parents and all other caretakers, having a better idea of how kids develop and perceive the world allows us to speak and listen more effectively.

FACTORS THAT IMPACT CHILD PSYCHOLOGY

Childhood development is influenced by a number of different internal and external factors. You have probably heard of the old "nature vs. nurture" debate, which aims to determine whether our personalities are a product of genetics or their environment.

Psychologists tend to agree on a midway point between the two extremes. Kids can be influenced both by their nature *and* the way they are nurtured. However, more weight is usually given to the impact of the "nurture" side of the equation, in part because we can change it.

When discussing child psychology, internal factors that influence child psychology can be defined as anything a child was born with innately. Typically, this means characteristics determined solely by genetics. These factors and their impact on child development are difficult if not impossible to change because they are instinctual. There is very little anyone can do to change our child's genes once they are born.

External factors, on the other hand, impact your child's personality after birth. It is easier to recognize how factors like socialization and family life might influence how your child sees the world. Just as a certain experience might help us see life in a different light, so too can our kids. In fact, kids are often even more affected by their experiences and environments than adults because kids are still developing.

In child psychology, there are three major contexts that are recognized as having a significant impact on development: cultural, social, and socioeconomic.

Cultural Context

Culture consists of the unique behaviors, activities, and lifestyles in a certain population. We tend not to notice these traits in our own culture because we are so used to it. However, if we travel to other countries or states, we often find that our cultural norms are different or nonexistent there. It can be very hard to immerse ourselves fully in a new culture once we're adults, whether it's a vacation or a permanent move, simply because we are so accustomed to our own.

Culture can vary significantly from region to region, and what's normal in one culture may be abnormal or even frowned upon by another. For example, in some cultures giving a thumbs up signifies that the recipient did well, while in others it's actually a rude gesture. Food, art, and education also vary widely.

Common discipline methods for kids can differ too. Each of these differences has an impact on the kids that grow up in these cultures. The way kids relate to their parents, the type of child care we provide, and the education they get at school and at home are all products of our culture, so it's important to recognize what kind of lessons our culture teaches our still-developing kids.

Societal Influences and Expectations

The way kids are socialized has a powerful effect on personality and disposition. Forming healthy relationships with family and friends is an essential part of this process. Kids who don't spend a lot of time around their peers may struggle to practice their communication skills, often falling behind and having trouble identifying and expressing emotions. They may also have difficulty managing conflict if they haven't built up these skills, or if they are surrounded by examples of poor conflict management like arguing and physical violence. Kids often internalize the behaviors they see as well as the ones they experience firsthand. Providing your child with positive examples of healthy relationships and assisting them as they begin interacting with other kids and teachers helps them develop good communication skills and healthy relationships of their own.

Socioeconomic Factors

Socioeconomic factors include a family's social class, their financial situation, their jobs, where they live, and the education options that are available.

Each of these three factors plays an important role in child development. For example, if a family doesn't have much money and lives somewhere with poor public education, their child may struggle more than their more well-off peers. They may not be able to address any educational gaps at home if their parents or caretakers work long hours. Further issues may arise if kids lack access to sufficient nutrition and health care.

Of course, parents can raise a happy, healthy child even if they aren't rich. While kids who grow up in low-income households may have fewer opportunities than some of their peers, positive experiences with social and cultural contexts can help make up the difference. Still, it's important to account for the influence of socioeconomic status in child development. When you recognize how these factors come into play, you will better understand the needs of your child and what you can do to help fulfill those needs.

AREAS OF CHILD DEVELOPMENT

Now that you know the different contexts that influence child psychology, you can see how they contribute to child development. The three main areas of child development are physical, cognitive, and emotional. A healthy child should develop in each of these areas. Keeping an eye on your own child's physical, cognitive, and emotional skills can help ensure they're getting everything they need for regular development in each area.

In order to know if your child's development is on track, you must first know what's expected of them at each stage and area of child development. Let's take a look at the different areas now.

Physical

Your child's physical development typically follows a predictable series of events. Babies will learn to pick their heads up and roll over, and as your child progresses into the toddler stage they will begin to crawl, walk, and run with confidence and less risk of overbalancing and falling over.

Most kids learn to walk between one and two years old, so by the time your child is three or older, they should have relative mastery over these basic movements, barring any health conditions that might delay their physical development.

In some cases, issues with physical development can point to future troubles in cognitive and emotional development. Some kids are simply slower walkers than others, but occasionally these issues are more serious than your child simply being a late bloomer. If you notice significant delays in your child's physical abilities, speak to their doctor about possible causes and how this might impact other areas of development.

Cognitive

Cognitive development refers to the way your child thinks and perceives the world around them. Even as babies, kids generally show interest in their environment—for example, a baby might watch the spinning mobile above their head and follow its movements with their eyes. As kids continue to grow older, their cognitive abilities improve. They'll start to retain information, whether through something taught to them or something learned through experience. They'll also start using their imagination, problem-solving, and critical-thinking skills. These are important skills for communication and conflict resolution, as they allow kids to understand what they're being told and decide how they're going to react to that information.

Emotional

A child's emotional development is how well they are able to feel, recognize, and display their emotions. The older your child gets, the more complex these emotions will be, and the more trouble they may have understanding them. Simple emotions like anger and happiness are fairly easy to grasp and express, but complex ones like guilt and confidence may prove to be more confusing. You can assist in this process by encouraging your child to be honest and open about their emotions. Let them attempt to explain how they feel, and try not to discredit these emotions, even when they may not be appropriate for the situation. Through understanding their own feelings, kids are better able to regulate emotional expression as they grow up. They also get better at recognizing others' emotions and reacting to them accordingly. For example, a child with a high level of emotional development might see another child who is upset and try to comfort them. This showcases their ability to not only realize the signs of sadness but practice compassion and understanding.

Emotional development is closely related to a child's social skills. The more emotionally mature your child is, the better they will handle interpersonal conflicts. It can be tough for some kids to learn to understand,regulate, and appropriately manage their emotions. It's common for young kids to get upset to the point of tears at the idea of sharing their toys or playing the game someone else wants to play. However, practicing these skills through various forms of social interaction will teach them how to compromise, share, and collaborate to make and maintain relationships. A lack of adequate socialization can lead to problems with a child's emotional development. With good examples of healthy relationships and enough opportunities to socialize, kids will have an easier time grasping concepts like friendship, trust, and respect for authority figures like parents and teachers.

WHY UNDERSTANDING CHILD PSYCHOLOGY IS IMPORTANT

Understanding the psychology that influences your child's actions can help you be a better parent, guardian, or educator. By understanding your child's needs, you can ensure you're meeting those needs. It also allows you to speak to kids in a way they understand. If you're trying to explain to a toddler why they need to go to bed on time, they probably won't understand if you tell them it's because they need to maintain a good sleep cycle for healthy brain function.

Breaking this information down into something they can more easily understand will help you convince them to respect bedtime rules. For example, you might tell them that if they go to bed now, they'll have more energy to play with their friends tomorrow. This is something they can understand that will motivate them to follow your rules. Child psychology can also help you recognize reasons why your child might act differently than others. If they have different cultural or socioeconomic contexts, they might lack some of the opportunities other kids get and therefore could develop more slowly. By recognizing your child's unique needs, you can address them more appropriately and effectively.

Of course, it is always possible that your child is an outlier and doesn't follow some of the expected behavior and development timelines. This isn't necessarily a bad thing; the common knowledge we have about when and how kids develop is based on averages, which means there are as many kids who advance quicker than there are who advance slower. Recognizing these averages simply provides a frame of reference to help better understand our kids. If we notice that their development in a certain area is falling behind those averages, we can better identify contributing factors. This allows us to account for potential difficulties and focus on improving these underdeveloped areas.

Understanding child psychology also gives you a better idea of your child's perspective on issues. An outburst may seem completely random and unprovoked, but it might make more sense when you consider how your child's psychology differs from your own. They might lack the ability to regulate their emotions the same way adults do, so anything that makes them feel a little upset could potentially lead to an outburst. When you understand where your child is coming from and why they might be reacting the way they are, it's easier to push aside the frustration you might feel at the outburst and resolve the issue.

Finally, having a basic grasp of child psychology will help you set reasonable behavioral expectations and rules. Without it, you might establish rules that your child has no hope of following at their current developmental stage. For example, if your child's memory is still developing, it might be unfair to expect them to remember to follow rules you haven't mentioned to them in a while. If you account for this possibility, you can make sure to remind them of the rule when it becomes relevant again, and you can temper your frustration if they forget and the rule gets broken. Less anger leads to better communication and helps your kids correct their mistakes without feeling afraid or hurt by your reaction.

How to Better Understand Your Child

You can use child psychology to improve your understanding of your child's wants and needs. By giving your child the tools they need to develop and address any issues when they arise, you set the stage for better understanding between the two of you and better communication. Here are a few tips for getting to know your child and the way they think, feel, and react to their surroundings.

Spend Quality Time Together

One of the most reliable ways to encourage development and bond with your child is to simply spend time with them. If you often find yourself busy with work or other activities that separate you from your child, try to make a concerted effort to block off time for them. Ask them questions about their day and let them talk about what interests them. You can support this by asking specific questions that invite them to give a more detailed answer. Instead of simply asking if they had a good day, you might ask them what kind of games they played with their friends or the drawing they made. This kind of language invites kids to open up and show enthusiasm for what they like and dislike, which can give you more insight into who your child is as a person and the best strategies for communication. Avoid making judgments about your child's fears and insecurities, as kids are especially susceptible to discouragement at this point in their development. Even if you don't mean to, laughing at or brushing off a source of fear could cause them to feel embarrassed, and next time they might not feel comfortable discussing their fears with you.

Pay Attention to Environmental Factors

Another good method for understanding your child is to pay attention to their environment. Consider their home life, school, and any extracurricular programs or clubs they might be part of. Watch out for any potential negative influences, like arguments at home or community disputes that your child might pick up on. Even though you might assume these kinds of things would go right over your child's head, kids are often more perceptive (not to mention impressionable) than we believe. Identifying these negative influences could help explain why your child is having issues with aggression or shyness.

The more time you spend with your child and the more attention you are able to give them, the deeper the parent-child bond will become. Paying attention to their development—and understanding its psychological underpinnings—will help you lay the foundation for good communication.

2

BECOME THE MASTER OF YOUR EMOTIONS

It's important to understand your child's mind, but it's also important to understand your own mind. As the old adage goes, communication is a two-way street. If you want your child to listen to you, you have to be willing to listen to them, and you also need to know how to communicate effectively. One of the biggest roadblocks for communication between kids and parents is anger.

Anger can turn a productive discussion into an argument that helps no one. When we get angry, we get defensive, and we become worse at explaining our point of view. Instead, we start trying to 'win' the argument. But when we're talking to our kids, there should be no winners or losers. We are just trying to get them to understand what we want them to do, not to debate them. If we resort to yelling and lose control of ourselves, we tend to resort to the dreaded "because I said so." Our kids may also be less likely to listen to us because they get defensive at our raised tone of voice, just like we would get defensive if someone yelled at us. They stop listening to what we're saying, and we stop saying much more than "listen to me or else."

Needless to say, this isn't any way to hold a productive conversation. If we want our kids to listen, we have to learn to control our anger when we talk to them. We can't get so wrapped up in the "argument" that we end up in a screaming match with our own kids, and we definitely don't want to say anything cruel that we'll regret later. In order to communicate with our kids, we need to learn to recognize sources of our own anger, readjust our thinking, and develop practices for calming us down when we feel we're on the verge of screaming. Deescalating the conversation lets you more effectively convince your child to listen, and it helps you better manage any tantrums your child may throw during the discussion.

ANGER TRIGGERS

Anger is a strong emotion that we tend to express before we even recognize we're feeling it. It can bubble up inside us quickly, causing us to say things we don't mean just because we're lashing out at someone. While it can be hard to stop ourselves from reacting in anger in the heat of the moment, we can make it easier for ourselves by learning to recognize our anger triggers. If we can anticipate when we'll feel angry, we can address these potential issues and calm down more effectively.

Anger triggers are the experiences, activities, and phrases that are most likely to make us angry. We encounter many different anger triggers throughout the day. These might include general things like getting stuck in traffic or speaking to a rude customer or coworker at your job. These kinds of triggers are likely to make anyone angry. There are also more specific anger triggers that reflect your personal pet peeves and insecurities. For example, if you're someone who has trouble feeling listened to in your life, you might get more upset at getting talked over than someone who hasn't had the same experiences. Our individual anger triggers can come from our lifestyles, our previous experiences, and even past traumas. However, just because these events are capable of making us angry doesn't mean we have to give in to that anger. If we learn to recognize and anticipate our anger when we come into contact with anger triggers, we can regain control over ourselves and calm down much faster than if these triggers catch us off guard.

Common Anger Triggers for Parents

As parents, there are many behaviors our kids can engage in that might make us angry. We love our kids, but that doesn't mean they can never upset us. We might feel frustrated when they don't listen, upset when they're not doing well at school, or hurt if they attack us.

Some of the behaviors our kids do that commonly lead to anger include talking back, whining, crying, yelling, bickering with friends or siblings, having a meltdown, and acting stubborn. These behaviors are more likely to make us mad if we're already in a stressful situation, such as running late to an important event, or dealing with their fussy siblings. We can also feel a sort of protective rage if someone hurts or upsets our kids, and we may inadvertently project some of this anger onto the child. For example, if our child nearly has a dangerous accident, we might turn our anger on them rather than the person or object that would have hurt them. While we may only be reacting this way because we care about their safety, all the child sees is our anger.

Being a parent is a stressful job, and it's one that comes with many upsides but also plenty of aggravation. The previously discussed examples are all common triggers for anger, and it's natural to feel this way when these events occur. But just because the feelings themselves are understandable doesn't mean that it's acceptable to express these feelings by yelling or retaliating. In order to shift how we express our anger as parents, we must first understand why these triggers make us so angry.

. . .

How to React to These Triggers

Reframing the way we think about and understand our anger can help us manage it. One of the biggest underlying causes of anger in parents is a sense of inadequacy. We want to be the best parents we can be, and when our kids act out or don't excel in school and relationships, we may take this as a sign that we have failed as parents. To be sure, parenting is tough, especially if you are a first-time parent. We're often not entirely sure what the best way to raise our kids is, and because of this, we can feel inadequate and defensive if we start thinking we're parenting them wrong. Oftentimes, "Feelings of inadequacy occur when we are jarred out of preconceived notions of what kids need, what they should be like, or how they ought to respond to us" (Stosny, 2015, para. 5). If our child acts differently than we would expect them to—ie, in a way that doesn't align with our ideas of how a well-adjusted, healthy child should act—we tend to take this as a referendum on our parenting skills. It can make us feel vulnerable, which activates the fight-or-flight response and, in some cases, full-blown anger.

Feelings of inadequacy tend to morph into anger when we stop seeing our kids as individuals and instead focus on how they "should be" acting. Each child has his or her own individual needs and personality. As parents, it's our job to adapt our parenting style to suit these needs, and to gently encourage our kids to grow and develop into happy, healthy adults.

If your child is acting out and you feel yourself getting angry, consider whether the anger is really warranted or whether you're really just feeling defensive about your parenting. To be sure, there are some behaviors from kids that are unacceptable, but trying to correct these behaviors by getting angry at your child isn't a productive way to go about it. You can always adjust your parenting style until you find one that works well for you and your child. Take time to listen to what your child needs, and take a moment to calm yourself down before you address your child's anger.

HANDLING TANTRUMS WITHOUT ANGER

When kids throw tantrums, our initial response is often aggravation. Maybe we're somewhere public, and the last thing we want is for our child to have a meltdown in the middle of the grocery store, or a place where they're supposed to be quiet. Maybe we're rushing around and we know stopping and addressing the issue is only going to make us even later than we already are. Maybe we've had a long day at work, we're exhausted, and we just want to relax, so our child's outburst feels like just one more annoyance on the ever-growing pile.

Whatever we might have been doing before the tantrum began, that characteristic wailing and stomping is never a good sign. It's a huge source of stress, and if we're around other people when it happens, we might fear being judged. Taken altogether, it's no wonder we tend to get angry when our kids throw tantrums.

Frustration might be understandable, but that doesn't mean it's the best response. When we're stressed and tense, our kids are too. When we're terse with them, they notice. This can trigger a meltdown, or make it harder to stop one once it's already in progress. Rather than de-escalating the situation, we might unthinkingly make things worse by raising our voices and punishing kids for their tantrums. This doesn't teach our kids emotional management skills, nor does it help us manage the conflict. The best way to handle a temper tantrum is to first calm yourself down, and then calm your child down. In order to do this, it helps to have a better understanding of why your child is throwing a tantrum in the first place and what you can do to handle it in a level-headed way.

Why Kids Throw Tantrums

While you may know some adults who seem to have mood swings as uncontrollable as kids do, temper tantrums are much more common in young kids. As adults, we have the vocabulary necessary to express our emotions with our words. We also have years of practicing the emotional maturity skills necessary for proper communication. Whether your emotional maturity is top-notch or a little rusty, you have still gone through all the mental development necessary to regulate your emotions. However, kids have not. As we discussed in the previous chapter, kids are still undergoing a lot of mental development at this stage, including the parts of their brains that help them manage their emotions. Because of this, they tend to be more prone to angry outbursts and tears when there's a conflict or disturbance to their routine.

It can be hard for us to understand why kids throw tantrums, especially when we're thinking about them like tiny adults. We watch our kids ball up their fists and start crying after their favorite show ends and we think, "Why are they so upset? Don't they know it's not such a big deal?" Of course, the problem is that kids don't know this. They often don't understand that these issues, which seem major in their minds, are very minor in the grand scheme of life because they haven't had the life experiences to tell them that. Their life is only what they have experienced so far, so something as small as the wrong show playing on TV is a big deal. On top of this, kids lack the language needed to communicate their distress in any other way. They often resort to crying, yelling, throwing, or hitting because these are the only ways they know to make an impact on the world around them. This kind of behavior is more likely to continue if we reaffirm this belief. If, however, we give them tools to express themselves another way, and we don't let the volume of their voice dictate our response to their tantrum, we can encourage our kids to handle their anger more appropriately.

When we understand that kids throw tantrums because they lack the knowledge and skill to express themselves the way adults might—not because they're being spiteful or want to be a problem—we're better at keeping our anger out of the picture. We can be reasonable in our approach to our kids' anger without adding our own anger to the mix. Instead of getting mad at our kids for acting out, we see the situation as an opportunity to prevent future tantrums. This level-headed approach keeps us from escalating the tantrum or saying something that could at best upset our kids further, and at worst stick with them long after the tantrum. We must recognize that while tantrums aren't completely unavoidable, especially in early childhood, we can still help our kids get a handle on their emotions and teach them how to process these feelings early on in life.

Our goal during a tantrum should be not just to get our kids to stop crying but to help them learn to calm themselves. We must teach kids the best way to express their sadness and anger, and we must encourage them to use their words to explain how they feel rather than jumping right to a meltdown. Through this, we will expand their emotional maturity and ensure future meltdowns are more manageable.

Why You Should Stay Calm

Kids often learn more from us than we think. They listen, watch, and emulate what we say and do. They can pick up on cues in our behavior that they then internalize and practice themselves, even if it's a behavior we'd rather they avoid. We can be a positive influence on our kids just as easily as a negative influence. If we practice kindness, compassion, and good listening skills, our kids will pick up on these. If our kids watch us share our possessions with family and neighbors, they become better at sharing with their friends. If they see us at our jobs, they might pretend to work too, even if their understanding of what we actually do at work is a little skewed.

In many cases, we pass along good lessons to our kids this way, or at least get a lighthearted chuckle out of their attempts to play pretend. But we can pass along bad behaviors in the same way. If our kids see and hear us argue with our spouse, they learn all the mean things people say to each other when they're mad. They internalize the idea that it's okay to shout and slam things when we're mad if they see us do it first. The concept of "do as I say, not as I do" doesn't really exist for kids. No matter what we tell them to do, if we don't practice what we preach, they're not going to fully get it.

Nowhere is it more important to practice good values than when we are interacting directly with our kids. When we are face to face with our kids, they pick up even more about our body language and tone. If we sound stressed and angry, they'll subconsciously pick up on these cues and become stressed and angry themselves. Their minds tell them there is something to get upset about, so they do, even if they otherwise wouldn't have escalated the tantrum.

If instead we take a moment to calm ourselves down, they'll pick up on that. They will understand there's nothing to fear in their current situation, and they will stop working themselves up as soon as we show them it's okay to be calm. Once they've internalized your lack of anger, they can let their own anger go, at which point you can ask them to express how they're feeling with their words.

Remaining calm also sets a good example for our kids. If we can stay level-headed in the face of a source of stress, they will copy that behavior, and they'll start to manage sources of stress in their own life in the same way. If we show them that anger or even violence are acceptable solutions, they'll copy these behaviors instead. We want to set the best example we can for our kids, so we should always try to act how we would want them to act. By taking a minute to cool off and talking about our emotions openly with them, they learn that it is okay to do the same thing, whether they're upset with us, another family member, or one of their friends.

How to Calmly Handle Tantrums

You now know why it's so important to stay calm, but it can still be hard to actually put this into practice. We are only human, after all, and it can be hard for us to not leap immediately to frustration when our kids do things that upset us. In the middle of a temper tantrum, it's easy to lose our cool and end up acting exactly how we know we shouldn't. In order to stay calm during tantrums, here are a few steps you can follow to address the issue appropriately and some tips for redirecting your anger in a way that won't interfere with your ability to have a conversation with your child.

Take a Breather

Breathing is an invaluable tool for managing anger. When we purposefully calm our breathing, we can back away from the angry feelings stewing inside us and reaffirm control over them. Simple breathing exercises may not seem like much, but they're surprisingly effective. Our breathing rate is connected to our heart beat, our blood pressure, and even our natural response to stress. When we hyperventilate by taking too many quick, shallow breaths, we work ourselves up. By slowing our breathing, we return our pulse and blood pressure to normal, which takes us out of fight or flight mode and helps us deal with problems more effectively.

When you catch yourself getting upset, try not to react right away. Delay the reaction by counting backward from 10 in your head. The time it takes you to get to "one" is enough time for you to reevaluate your response. If you still feel out of balance, take some slow, deep breaths—in through your nose and out through your mouth. Feel the way the air enters and exits your body, and imagine your stress leeching away with each breath. Breathe in and out in steady, even counts until you feel you can manage your anger.

. . .

Listen—Even if You Disagree

Discussions tend to turn into arguments when we don't listen to what the other person is saying. This is as true for conversations with our kids as it is for conversations with other adults.

Failing to listen to your child will only make their tantrum worse, which only increases your headache. If kids feel like you're belittling their feelings, making fun of them, or punishing them for feeling a certain way rather than correcting how they express that feeling, they might be more reluctant to talk to you about their emotions in the future. If they feel like you're talking over them, they can start to yell louder just so they feel like they're heard. In order to communicate with your child, you must listen to them and try to understand why they feel the way they do. This lets them feel like their feelings are validated, which can help them return to a calmer state.

Of course, this doesn't mean you have to agree with them, nor does it mean you should never correct behavior that goes too far. If your child hits you or someone else, if they continue to raise their voice, or if they destroy property, you still need to tell them that what they did was wrong. If they refuse to go to bed even though it's bedtime, it's still important for your child to obey the rules. You shouldn't feel the need to abolish bedtime just because you want to show your child you're listening.

However, you should at least listen to their points of view before determining the best course of action. If the kids don't want to go to bed, ask them why. Maybe they have an activity they want to do, or maybe they aren't sleepy because they're stressed out about something happening tomorrow. Once they start talking to you instead of yelling, and once you've heard what they have to say, you can reward this behavior and come up with an offer that helps them feel heard while sticking to your rules. For example, maybe you could remind them that if they clean their room, they can do that fun activity they wanted to do in the morning. Or, the sooner they get their homework done, the sooner they get to play video games. If they're dreading something tomorrow, ask them why they're worried and how you can help. This shows your child you're listening and willing to compromise. You are still the one in charge, but your child gets rewarded for talking to you about their problems instead of having a meltdown.

Teach Coping Mechanisms

While tantrums are never something we would actively encourage, they do make for great teaching moments. When your child's emotions get the best of them, and when your emotions threaten to do the same, you have an opportunity to change this pattern of behavior for you both. Teach your child how to cope with their emotions so they are less to throw a tantrum in the future.

The kind of coping mechanism that works best for you or your child will vary. Some people respond very well to taking deep breaths. Practicing meditation can also help when you feel emotionally conflicted. Others find that a calming activity like reading or drawing can help them let go of their residual agitation.

Sometimes coping mechanisms can be more physical in nature. For example, you could ask your child to do five jumping jacks when they feel themselves getting angry. This helps them burn off excess energy while bringing a bit of fun to the proceedings. After all, it's hard to argue with someone when you're jumping and flailing your hands in the air. Try out a few different coping methods until you find one that effectively reduces anger.

When we reframe these tantrums as teachable moments, it becomes easier to deal with them and to talk our kids out of them. We can set aside our own frustration and instead focus on helping our kids rather than getting mad at them for things they can't quite control yet. The longer we practice these anger management strategies during tantrums, the fewer tantrums they will have.

STRATEGIES FOR MANAGING YOUR ANGER

Dealing with tantrums isn't the only time our anger might threaten to get the best of us. There are plenty of parenting experiences that can induce anger, frustration, and even rage if we're not careful about how we express our feelings. As a reminder, it's okay and natural to feel this way from time to time. If we have an aggravating or annoying experience, it's not surprising that we might feel angry. On top of that, it's not healthy to pretend we aren't feeling anger and shove it down inside us.

Still, just as we teach our kids when we correct their tantrums, there are acceptable and unacceptable ways to express that anger and unacceptable ways, especially in regards to how we expose our kids to our own anger. Remaining calm in difficult situations and redirecting anger in non-destructive ways are critical lessons if you are looking for a calmer parenting style.

By adopting strategies for anger management, you improve communication between you and your child.. You can demonstrate all the skills they need to center themselves in moments of agitation. In managing your own anger, you also manage your child's anger without any additional effort.

Change up Your Morning Routine

We tend to be in better moods when we start our days off right. They don't call being in a bad mood "waking up on the wrong side of the bed" for nothing!

The way we begin our day has a huge impact on how we feel the rest of the day. If we roll out of bed late, begin the day by fighting with our kids about getting ready, and automatically assume we're going to have bad experiences, we will definitely allow our self-fulfilling prophecy to come true. We'll end up stuck in a cycle of negativity that contributes to stress and more bouts of anger.

In order to eliminate this early-morning stress, we must shake up our mornings and start them out on the right foot. If you find yourself rushing around trying to get everything ready before everyone goes off to school or work, try shifting your sleep schedule so you go to bed half an hour earlier and wake up half an hour earlier. With the extra time, you can more comfortably manage all of your morning responsibilities. You'll also likely feel better rested by going to sleep a little earlier, meaning you'll have enough energy to calmly deal with a fussy child in the morning.

If you want to add a little more zen to your morning routine, plan a small, relaxing but fun activity for right after you wake up. Instead of rolling out of bed and scrambling to get ready, try taking just fifteen minutes to read a book or do a brief stretching exercise. You might even dedicate your morning to getting a workout in before everyone else is up and ready to distract you from your yoga or a quick jog around the block. Do something that centers your mind and energizes you, making you excited to wake up rather than dreading it. This makes it easier to go to bed in the evenings, as you know you always have something good to look forward to each day. If you start your morning out on this positive note, it sets the tone for the rest of the day.

It can be hard to find time for a real breakfast in the mornings. We may find ourselves rushing around and grabbing something unhealthy while hardly saying a word to our family. This can negatively impact our mood and overall health. If you can wake up a little early, use this extra time to make yourself and your family a real breakfast so you can eat together and bond at the breakfast table. Alternatively, adults could practice intermittent fasting, which typically involves skipping breakfast and only eating during certain windows each day. This has also been linked to some notable health benefits like weight loss and higher energy levels throughout the day. Either method is better than grabbing an unhealthy breakfast and rushing out the door, so try them both and see which works best for you and your family. The key is not to follow any particular diet but to try things out and find a healthful, positive routine everyone can stick with and enjoy over time.

Try Out Routine Meditation

We've already discussed the benefits of doing breathing exercises while we're in the heat of the moment, but it's also a good idea to turn meditation into part of your daily routine. It's a great addition to your early morning habits, but it can also be helpful to calm your mind shortly before bed, helping you shed the stresses of the day. Meditation has significant long-term benefits for our mentalities and outlooks on life. It teaches us to be more in tune with our breathing and our emotional state, which helps us be more mindful of our thoughts and feelings. Studies have shown that people who meditate consistently are more successful at "reducing stress, improving sleep, increasing focus, [and] improving relationships" (Headspace, n.d., para. 1). These are all great benefits if you're trying to live a more peaceful life and reduce the presence of volatile emotions that could harm your ability to communicate with your child.

You can practice a very simple meditation just by finding a calm, quiet place, closing your eyes, and focusing on your breath. After a few minutes of deep breathing, you'll feel more focused and centered. After a few days, you'll have a better grasp on your emotions, as well as how you can recognize them and change how you express them. If you're not especially great at holding yourself to meditation and you need some additional help, look for guided meditations online. You can find everything from general meditation routines to more specific routines on topics like gratitude, dealing with anger, or manifesting success. Whatever type of meditation you choose to practice, you'll get all the upsides that meditation can bring as long as you stick to it for just a few minutes each day.

Address Your Wants and Needs

As parents, we often get so wrapped up in our kids' wants and needs that we forget our own. We see them as less important than making sure our kids are attended to. However, unfulfilled wants and needs can interfere with our ability to be effective parents. If stress and anxiety are weighing us down, we'll be distracted and more prone to snapping in stressful situations. Our exhaustion and aggravation piles up. We need time to ourselves to decompress and unwind just like everyone else. This means taking time to do fun, enriching activities that alleviate stress on top of our other parenting duties.

Of course, while a spa day or a vacation might sound nice, parenting is a job that doesn't come with sick days or vacation hours. It can be hard to find the time to address our needs. If you're having difficulty staying refreshed and rejuvenated, there are a few solutions you can try to work around your kid's schedule. The first is to schedule "me time" for when your child is otherwise occupied. This might mean in the evenings after they go to bed, or during the day while they're at school, if you're not working during these hours. Even if you are, enjoying a nice lunch or chatting with coworkers can help you replenish some of your energy. If you have a spouse, partner, or someone else who is sharing parenting duties with you, make sure they're pulling their weight. If you're being saddled with the brunt of the parenting responsibility, you're going to get exhausted after a while, and you might even feel resentful of your partner. If you need to, have an honest conversation about how much effort they're making to raise your child and what you'd like to see them do to be more present in your child's life. When your spouse picks up some of the slack, this can leave you with more free time to decompress.

Your spouse isn't the only person who can watch your child for a while if you need to take a break. Ask other members of the family if they'd be willing to watch the kids for a while. You could also look into daycare services or enlist the help of a neighborhood babysitter. Even if you only for a few hours, you are giving yourself the opportunity to recharge your parenting batteries. Don't feel bad about needing some time to yourself. It doesn't make you a bad parent to still want to see a movie or read a book without having to rush away to put out a fire. So long as you remain present in your child's life, there's nothing wrong with taking a break every once in a while.

Finally, you can also seek out activities that you can do together with your child to let off a little steam. While kids can be a source of significant stress, more often than not they are still the light of our lives. Spending time with them can bring us joy just as much as spending time with our friends or other family members. If you need some time to destress, take your child to the movies, or go out to eat with them. Play a game together, solve a puzzle, or read to them. The list of activities that are fun for both parents and kids is endless, and engaging in these kinds of activities can strengthen your parent-child bond.

SET REALISTIC EXPECTATIONS

A common pitfall when trying to manage our anger comes in the form of setting our expectations too high for our kids. This means we expect too much of them for the amount of cognitive development they have experienced so far. We might expect our kids to remember rules we have laid down or routines we've established for them, but truly acquiring the skill or knowledge can take more practice than we might think. They may not fully understand what we're asking, or they might have trouble keeping their emotions in check if they're not old enough to master those skills yet. It's important for us to be patient with both our kids and ourselves. Some lessons will only take a few hours or days to learn, while others might take weeks or months of practice. If we go in with this mindset, we'll have a lot more patience when certain lessons take time for kids to internalize.

We might also put a lot of pressure on our kids to do well in school or an extracurricular activity. If our kids aren't great at math right away, or if they're not the star of their little league team, we might feel disappointed. We may even question our parenting skills, again falling into the trap of feeling insecure about ourselves and lashing out in anger as a result. We might get mad at our kids because we expect better grades or better performance, even though we know they're trying their best.

This can blind us to possible alternative solutions to these problems, like tutoring, extra practice at home, and different methods of teaching. When we learn to manage expectations and accept our kids for who they are, we can help them improve without putting the burden of shame and failure on their shoulders, or on our own. Try to set realistic expectations for your kid's behaviors and achievements and make adjustments only if kids aren't quite hitting these reasonable goals.

Improving our communication skills and our relationships with our kids starts with improving ourselves. When we manage our expectations, adjust our emotions, and moderate our own tempers, we set a good example for our kids and help them do the same. With these skills, we are ready to help our kids master their emotions and have clear and positive conversations with us.

3

THE MISSING STEP IN MOST PARENTING RELATIONSHIPS

There are plenty of issues that can damage the relationship between parent and child. These issues might come in the form of a lack of trust, such as if your child lies to you about whether they broke something or the dog did it, or if your child doesn't feel they can trust you. Another common issue is a lack of understanding for each other. If you're not listening to what the other person has to say, you're not making an effort to meet them halfway as you would in other life conflicts. You may also have trouble laying down rules and getting kids to follow them, or getting your child to respect your authority as a parent without using methods that make them afraid of you. Each of these issues has the potential to damage or complicate the relationship between you and your child, which has the potential to harm their development.

If these issues aren't corrected early in a child's development, they can persist long into their teen and young-adult years, if not for the rest of their lives. Our early years have a huge part in determining who we're going to be as adults. If the way you interact with your younger child causes mistrust, you may end up with a teenager who is more likely to act out in destructive ways. They may embrace risky behaviors, and they misbehave even further if you react by tightening the reins without speaking to them about the issue. If you don't try to understand your child when they're young and you don't encourage them to open up to you, you may find your relationship fractured and distant later on. If you rely on strict punishments for bad behaviors rather than trying to talk about the issue and uncover the root of the problem, you may irreparably damage this relationship as your child grows to fear or even resent you. This is a frightening thing to think about for any parent, but if we allow ourselves to act out of uncontrolled anger and frustration, it could very well become a reality.

How do we fix these issues? How do we make sure we're giving our kids the best care we can, adequately preparing them for the rest of their lives? The key lies in looking at the common factor in all of the above issues: poor communication. A lack of communication is at the heart of these problems, and it will continue to bog down our personal relationships until we purposefully change the way we approach having a conversation with our kids. If we try to dominate the conversation, imposing our will and even threatening kids until they listen to us, we risk driving our kids away. If we never set any rules or boundaries, kids don't know what we expect from them, and they're more likely to keep pushing these invisible boundaries until they find the line they shouldn't cross. If we set boundaries but fail to appropriately convey these boundaries to our kids, any punishment we give them feels arbitrary and unearned in their eyes, because they don't know the rules. We haven't told them what those rules are. Whether we fail to set any rules, we fail to tell kids these rules or are too strict with our rules and don't let our kids be part of the conversation, we falter when it comes to communication. This sabotages our best efforts, all because we didn't understand how to talk to our kids.

While poor communication can be a serious problem in parent-child relationships, the good news is that it doesn't have to be this way. You can establish honest and clear communication with your child by changing your interactions with them. This single change will have a positive ripple effect that will eventually reach all areas of your child's life as they get older. Through first understanding the role of communication in your relationship with your child and then adopting strategies and habits that allow for good communication, you can strengthen your relationship and encourage your child's healthy development.

COMMUNICATION AND PARENTAL RELATIONSHIPS

If we've never spoken to someone before, we consider them a stranger. When we've talked to them a few times, they become an acquaintance. If there is compatibility, deeper and more personal conversations may lead to friendship. Developing relationships with our kids follows a similar pattern. If we don't communicate with kids, we remain "strangers," even if we live under the same roof. We don't get to really know our kids as individuals and deepen our bonds with them. It is only when we communicate with our kids that we begin to solidify the relationship.

Talking to our kids aids their development at every stage. Think back to when your child was a baby. They didn't understand what you were saying, but you probably still talked to them as if they could. Even though they might not know the meaning of the words, babies still pick up on our tone. They might ball up their fists and cry if they hear raised voices or a terse tone of voice, or they might giggle and smile along if our words are pleasant and playful. During these early months, our kids learn to communicate with us too.

They learn to tell us they're upset or scared by calling for us. They tell us they're curious and playful by moving their arms and legs. When a baby says their first word, it's typically treated as a momentous occasion, as it should be. This is proof that your child's communication skills are developing.

Now that our kids are older, we might not treat every new development milestone with the same gravitas. We probably don't make a scrapbook entry when our kids first talk to us about their feelings or resolve their first argument with a friend. But these moments are no less important, as communication is critical at every stage. Everything we teach our kids through the way we communicate with them is a lesson they internalize and emulate. If we pay attention to our kids' communication skills and the way we talk to them, we can see the direct impact of our words and actions on their development.

How Poor Communication Can Negatively Impact Development

Unfortunately, not all methods of communication are positive and healthy. If we struggle to communicate effectively with our kids, they could have trouble in various areas of their development.

We use language as a way to get to know each other. If we don't talk to each other, we may not ever fully understand who our kids are, and our kids can feel equally distant from us. They may be uncertain about being open and vulnerable with us because they haven't learned these skills. We don't form the same close connection that we could if only we knew how to listen and speak effectively. This may create a painful rift between parent and child that can, in some cases, keep kids from forming a genuine emotional bond with us.

We're not the only ones affected by communication issues. If we don't pass along the skills our kids need to form and maintain relationships with us, they can have difficulty forming and maintaining relationships with their peers. They may be unable to deal effectively with conflicts, and may resort to yelling or hitting to get their way. They may also have trouble speaking honestly to their friends, which can become an issue as kids get older and talk about more serious problems in their lives. If kids lack the skills necessary to connect to other kids their age, they may find themselves struggling to make friends and further develop their social skills. Additionally, they may have more trouble at school because they struggle with the communication skills necessary for education. They may not adequately develop the listening skills needed to pay attention in class, or they may have trouble communicating their thoughts and answering questions on homework and quizzes. Academic difficulties at an early age could continue well into their academic career if they never build up their communication skills.

Another area that is often negatively impacted by poor communication skills is self-esteem. Good communication and close bonds with friends can help ward off low self-esteem issues in kids. When kids struggle to make friends, or if they perform poorly in school as a result of their inability to listen, their self-confidence can suffer. Kids who have unaddressed communication needs "often see themselves as less able and less popular than their friends" (The Communication Trust, n.d., para. 7). Poor self-esteem in kids could keep them from reaching their full potential and living a happy life. It can contribute to mental health issues later in life and interfere with your child's ability to form healthy relationships in the future.

While each of these potential negative impacts can be scary to think about, it's important to know about them so you can take the steps necessary to avoid them. By building up your kids' communication skills, you ensure they're able to form a healthy parent-child relationship, as well as relationships with their friends and educators. This encourages their development and keeps them from falling behind other kids their age.

ADVANTAGES OF GOOD COMMUNICATION

If you can avoid the pitfalls of lackluster communication and instead practice good communication skills as a parent, the benefits are tremendous. For one, you get to avoid each of the unfortunate side effects of poor communication. This means kids are better at forming relationships and are more likely to do well in school. Kids who are taught good communication skills are also more likely to have a positive relationship with their parents. This positive relationship develops because kids understand what it means to be respectful in a relationship where both parties feel seen and heard. They also become more comfortable with their role in the family and the rules they're expected to follow. They understand more about themselves and their feelings, and they know when it's appropriate to act a certain way and when it's not.

As your child learns each of these lessons, they will start to see you not just as their parent but also as someone they can trust and rely on. They will look to you for advice, and they will be more likely to listen to you as long as you maintain this standard of effective communication. The simple arts of talking and listening pave the way for healthy development and healthy relationships for kids.

. . .

Building Mutual Respect

When most people think of respect in the parent-child dynamic, they generally think of kids being respectful toward their parents. To be sure, this is an important aspect of your relationship to establish. If your child doesn't respect you, they're not going to listen when you tell them to do things. They might question your authority, talk back, and go against your wishes because they feel like they "can." When your child respects you, they're more likely to listen even when they don't fully understand why you're asking them to clean up their toys or go to bed on time. However, the respect in your relationship shouldn't be one-sided. If you want your child to respect you, you also have to show them respect.

Just like in many other aspects of parenting, it is up to us to model the behaviors we want to see in our kids. If we want to show them how to be respectful, we must be respectful toward them too.

Many parents make the mistake of demanding respect from their kids without showing them the same courtesy. They see themselves as "the boss" and they want to be listened to without discussion or objection, but this just isn't how a healthy relationship works. While you will need to put your foot down as a parent, you can do this while still being respectful of your kid's needs, their boundaries, and their feelings. In fact, by showing your child respect, they will mimic your behavior. They'll be more receptive to your guidance and more willing to listen, all because you showed them they're worthy of your respect, and you're worthy of theirs.

One way to show your child the basics of respect is to give them autonomy. When kids are young, we want to do everything for them. We tend to resist the idea of letting our kids take care of themselves or make their own decisions. After all, we're the parents; we're responsible for their safety. This is fine when they're not old enough to make these choices themselves, but eventually our kids will start establishing boundaries for personal comfort and privacy. If we try to intrude upon these boundaries, often by being "helicopter parents" who insist kids wear a certain outfit, for example, or or talk over them in conversations. It's hard to relinquish this control, but we have to accept that our kids are learning and growing every day. If we don't give them the space to start making small decisions about their likes, dislikes, and what they're comfortable with, they're going to start feeling like we don't care about their feelings.

Encourage your child to start out by making small decisions for themselves. When they're old enough to get themselves dressed, let them choose between a few different outfits rather than just deciding on one yourself. Eventually, they'll be able to pick out clothes that help them express their unique personality and style, helping them affirm their sense of self. If possible, let your child have a space that is entirely their own, where they can go to cool down if they need to. This can help them feel more secure when they're still learning to control their emotions.

If they get themselves in trouble at school because of bad behavior, resist the urge to call up the teacher and bail them out. You can show them you sympathize, but it's important for them to take responsibility for their mistakes. Show them you value their opinions. They'll become more independent, not to mention more likely to treat you with respect. You'll form a bond based not on fear of your authority but on mutual respect and love, which is a far stronger force.

Helping Kids Understand Themselves

Growing up can be confusing for kids. They're constantly experiencing and learning about the world around them, and this information can be hard to process. Perhaps nothing is quite as difficult for kids to understand as themselves. Since kids' brains are still developing at this stage, their sense of self is continually developing too. They likely don't fully understand their own feelings and how to handle them, let alone who they are as a person. You can assist them in this process by helping them recognize and explain their feelings. When they're able to identify these feelings, they can take steps to react appropriately.

You can encourage greater emotional maturity for your child just by talking to them. If you notice your child getting upset, sit down with them and ask them to identify how they're feeling. If they're struggling, you can ask them, "Do you feel sad because of what happened? Did it make you angry?" You can provide the words they need to describe their feelings, but let them decide how they feel on their own. Once they do, help them understand what part of the situation made them feel that way. Maybe they got frustrated because they were trying to read something but couldn't sound out the words. If they got upset while playing, something about their game might have startled them.

Identifying the root of the problem in words is important for kids, even if the cause of their anger or sadness is obvious to you. They might not have made the connection, and they need frequent practice so they can start thinking about what made them feel a certain way. Then they can decide how they want to handle the emotion. Help them build their problem-solving skills by asking them what they think they should do to calm down, providing suggestions when necessary.

Finally, help them find a solution to the problem when you can. If they were getting frustrated trying to read, help them sound out the words that were giving them trouble. If they were bothered by something in their game, play with them for a bit or remove the thing that scared them. Remember: just because it seems trivial to you doesn't mean it is for your child. Try to think about being agitated yourself—then imagine a far more powerful person laughing at you or otherwise invalidating your feelings. This step shows your child that getting upset doesn't have to mean the situation is unsolvable. They can step away from the situation, calm down, ask for help, and return to the task

When you encourage your child to talk about their feelings, you also build up their self-esteem. If kids never feel in control of themselves, they can struggle with their self-esteem. They may also have a hard time interacting with other kids their age, which can contribute to feelings of loneliness and low self-worth. If they learn to understand their feelings, they will begin constructing a more stable sense of self. They will be able to decide how they react to their feelings and their social skills will improve. Each of these benefits helps them improve their self-esteem and feel more comfortable and in control of themselves.

Solidifying Your Relationship

Finally, improving communication between you and your child will improve your relationship. If you can't talk to each other and discuss your honest feelings about a situation, your relationship can suffer. If your child feels like they should hide things from you for fear of punishment, or if they strain the relationship by having constant tantrums and yelling to get their way, it's tough to have a bond deeper than a relatively surface-level connection. You might start to feel almost alienated from your child's life, and they might think of you as a distant parental figure rather than a warm and loving one.

When you have good communication, the barriers between the two of you fall away. You grow closer to each other and you genuinely enjoy spending time with your child and learning about the person they're becoming.

With good communication, you're able to listen to your kid's needs. This helps you more adequately address them. If your child is struggling in a certain area, like school or relationships, listen to what they say when they talk about these aspects of their life, then see if you can guide them toward an answer. If your child is argumentative, listen to why they disagree with you. Even if you remain firm in asking your child to do something they disagree with, as you must sometimes as a parent, you still show them that you consider their input when making a decision.

As a parent, you must clearly communicate your expectations. If kids don't know what's off-limits and what's okay, they won't be able to practice good behavior because they won't know what good behavior looks like. Remain consistent with your rules and make sure your child knows exactly what rules they should be following. This lets them better understand the expectations you've set and their expectations as a member of the family. They will become more cooperative, and when they behave badly they'll understand why that behavior was wrong and, by extension, that a reasonable, constructive correction may be justified. All of this leads to an improved relationship that is free of the stresses that plague other parental relationships. The only difference is communication.

SIMPLE TECHNIQUES FOR IMPROVING COMMUNICATION

We know now why communication matters, so let's put that knowledge into practice. We communicate with our kids dozens if not hundreds of times throughout the day, often nonverbally. This means we have plenty of opportunities to readdress our communication strategies and improve them. These changes don't have to be huge. They can be minor changes we make in the way we speak and listen each day.

We will go into more detail about methods for improving communication in later chapters. For now, we will just look at a few simple tricks and techniques you can use to improve communication with your child. Keep in mind that while each of these strategies can be helpful, they may not all be helpful for every child. You know your child best, so choose strategies you think they will respond to. Feel free to try out a few different strategies to determine which ones work best.

Show Interest

First and perhaps most importantly, you cannot be a passive listener. If your child is excited to tell you what happened at school today and you respond with half-hearted "uh-huhs" while they're talking, they're going to pick up on how disinterested you sound. If you continue to do another activity while they're talking like watching TV or working, you're not giving your child your full attention. This means you aren't really listening, which is a barrier to communication. Kids will pick up on this even if you try to be sneaky about checking your phone in the middle of their ramble. When your mind is elsewhere, your child learns that whatever they have to say isn't worth listening to. This can make them more reluctant to open up to you in the future.

It can often be hard to make time for our kids in the busy world we live in. Kids tend to barge in with little regard for whatever we are doing at the time. You might be overworked and stressed, but remember that your child doesn't fully understand this yet. All they see when you ignore their story in favor of your work is that they are less important to you, and this isn't the message you want to convey. Instead, either ask them to wait a moment while you finish up, or set your task down so you can give your child your attention. Don't pick it up again until the conversation is over. When appropriate, ask encouraging questions as they speak, less to learn more about the situation and more to let them know you're engaged in the story. This teaches kids that you care about what they have to say. It also helps you understand your child better, as you pay more attention to what they want to tell you about their day or their feelings.

Avoid Knee-Jerk Reactions

Poor communication is most common when we don't give ourselves time to process new information. We might react to bad news automatically, which can lead to us leaping right to anger and shouting before we've had a chance to cool off and think about the situation logically. This can leave us regretting our words and actions an hour later, when our emotions have calmed down and we realize we didn't react how we should have.

Let's consider an example to showcase how important it is to evaluate the situation before responding. Let's say your child comes home from school on the day they got their math test back. They hand it to you, and you see that they didn't do very well at all. You might be tempted to get angry at them for not paying attention in class or not trying their best. You might punish them by sending them to their room or revoking toy privileges until they improve their grades.

But what does this really teach your child? They learn to fear the idea of telling you about the struggles they're having in school. They learn that poor performance makes you angry and can lead to punishment. Next time they get a bad grade, they might try to hide it or lie about it. Punishing them for a bad grade doesn't actually help them improve their math skills, especially if your punishments target privileges that aren't contributing to the bad grade. These are all outcomes that you might have anticipated if you'd had a minute to think about the situation. If you react immediately upon seeing the test score, you're more likely to just yell and punish without thinking of the long-term consequences.

Now let's revisit the scenario. Let's say that instead of instantly getting angry and losing your temper, you take a moment to calm down before addressing the test score. You take a few deep breaths, and you remind yourself that there's no reason to get defensive over your parenting skills because of one bad test grade. Now, you might ask your child, "What parts of this test were hard for you? Can I help explain them to you? Why do you think you didn't do well?" If your child shows genuine interest in improving their grades with your support, praise their efforts, not just the results of those efforts. This time around, you're actually addressing the underlying causes of why the bad grade occurred, and you're creating a strategy for improving your child's focus. This will help them more in the long run than yelling ever would.

Encourage Your Child and Reinforce a Positive Self-Image

Regardless of how our kids behave, we still love them. We love the amazing people they are and the people we watch them become as they grow up and learn new things. The parent-child bond is incredibly strong, and it can withstand even the loudest temper tantrums. That being said, while our kids likely feel the same love toward us that we feel toward them, they might have trouble trusting us if we don't communicate this to them. Don't be afraid to tell your child things that might seem obvious from your perspective, such as that you love them and that you're proud of them. Kids need to hear these affirmations from time to time to really internalize them. They need to know that you're on their side no matter what. This can help fill in the gaps created by poor or unreliable communication. In that case, if you lose your temper and yell, your child will still know you love them and didn't mean to get so upset. You will be able to move on from the incident because you have made your child feel secure in your relationship with them.

It's also important to encourage and appreciate your child's efforts. If you can see they're putting a lot of effort into not losing their temper, thank them for being so patient and understanding, even if they slip up a little. Let them know when they do a good job, reinforcing this behavior—

acknowledging good behavior can be just as useful as criticizing bad behavior. Praise their efforts regardless of results. This teaches kids that making an effort is worth doing in and of itself. It also teaches them not to stress too much about perfection.

We are imperfect, flawed creatures, and it's okay for kids to mess up sometimes, just as we might mess up sometimes as parents. It doesn't make us bad people, and it doesn't make us unworthy of love. Mistakes are just a part of life, and it's okay for us and our kids to make them. Encourage your child to put in the effort to improve and show them you're happy to see their communication skills develop.

Involve Kids in Decision-Making When Appropriate

Finally, let kids know they have a voice and a say in what happens just like everyone else in the family. We sometimes have the desire to just tell kids what's happening and how we're going to do things without seeking or seriously considering their point of view. Rather than letting them express some agency, we tell them exactly how things are going to go and what they're going to do. When this doesn't align with what our kids want to do, they resist and create avoidable conflict. When you can, try to involve kids in the decision-making process, or at the very least explain to them why they have to do a certain action. Let them make small but not-insignificant choices and talk to them about why they're expected to act a certain way. When you do, kids will become better listeners, and they'll get experience making their own choices. This often makes them more responsible as they get older because they are used to making decisions and exercising their problem-solving skills.

Of course, not every decision can be left up to kids. If you let your child decide what you ate for every meal, you might end up having pizza and candy for dinner for an entire week. However, there are still many circumstances where it's important for kids to exercise their voice.

For instance, you can ask them how they like dinner and find out more about their food preferences. If they really like meatloaf but aren't a big fan of turkey, try to accommodate their preferences the same way you would accommodate your own.

Keep meals healthy, but try not to force kids to eat something they just don't like; instead, look for other options and encourage them to try new foods. You could ask what kind of vegetable they want with their meal. If kids choose a vegetable they like, they're more likely to eat it, which can help a lot with picky eaters. It also lets your child feel like they have some control over what they put into their body, and that you respect their opinions. This is the foundation of good communication with not just your child but anyone in your life.

4

SO HOW DO YOU GET YOUR CHILD TO LISTEN TO YOU?

Previously, we discussed strategies that involved learning how to listen to your child and adapt to their needs. We have covered how to resist anger and speak to our kids in a way they'll understand. We have focused on ourselves. Now, we're going to shift our focus to our kids and try to see things from their point of view.

We're going to take steps and implement strategies that encourage our kids to treat us with the same respect we're trying to show them. After all, it takes two active participants to have a conversation. If we're talking but our kids aren't listening, we're going to have the same communication issues we would have if our kids are talking and we weren't listening.

In this chapter, we'll cover a few different reasons why our kids might not be listening to us. We're also going to take a look at what we can do to resolve these issues when we encounter them, and how we can encourage our kids to be better listeners. It's important to note that the roadblocks to listening listed in this chapter do not account for any potential medical conditions or developmental disorders that might be impacting your child's ability to respond to directions. These issues can affect a child's hearing or their comprehension. If you believe your child may have one of these conditions, discuss the situation with a medical professional or child development specialist and follow their advice.

WHY KIDS MAY REFUSE TO LISTEN

Kids might not listen to us for a variety of different reasons. We tend to ascribe the behavior to plain old stubbornness or purposeful bad behavior. While kids are certainly capable of both , more often than not there is a reason behind their behavior. There is usually something keeping them from giving us their full attention, or there may be a previous incident that continues to influence how our kids are acting. These underlying causes can be hard to spot, especially if we are quick to jump to labeling it as simple defiance and even quicker to punish our kids for not listening. Taking a moment to try to identify the reasoning behind kids' stubborn or disrespectful behavior can help us deescalate a situation before it can turn into an argument. It also teaches us what conditions to look out for next time our kids are behaving badly so we can reduce the likelihood of the problem repeating itself.

Some of the reasons for a child's lack of listening skills have to do with how we talk to them and what we're saying. Other reasons might include what is currently going on around them, their own desires, and how we have acted in the past. Consider each of these areas as potential sources of stubborn behavior and try to identify which might be negatively influencing your child.

We Are Saying Too Much at Once

Kids aren't able to multitask or mentally juggle many things at once. If we give them too much to remember, they may struggle to keep up with it. For example, if you tell your child five or more rules at once, they might let one slip from their mind if they're not thinking about it. They might remember one or two, but they'll probably forget the others unless you make an effort to consistently remind them. It's not that they don't want to listen to you or obey your rules. Rather, they get overwhelmed and simply forget.

Imagine you're trying to tell your child to do a few chores around the house. Let's say that in one scenario, you give them the list of things to do all at the same time. You ask them to clean their room, pick up their toys in the living room, and get their laundry together to be washed. In the other scenario, you let them know you're going to ask them to do a few chores, but you assign the tasks one at a time and don't tell them to do the next task until they've finished the previous one. Which scenario do you think is going to turn out better? In the first one, your child might start cleaning up their room, but they'll probably get distracted before they can pick up their toys, let alone get their laundry together. In much the same way that you might forget to pick something up at the store if you don't have a way to reference your list, your child might forget the next task without meaning to. In the second scenario, there is no opportunity for your child to forget what's expected of them because you're not overloading them with directions. You're spelling things out for them in a clear and easy-to-follow way, and they're following through.

If you want your child to follow the rules, clarity and simplicity are key. Remind kids of the rules when you know they'll be relevant. For example, if you have a rule about no muddy shoes in the house, it's a good idea to restate this rule when it's raining and your child wants to go out and play. Repetition is a great way to make a complex list more easily memorized for kids. You can also try alternate memorization methods, like making a list and hanging it up on the wall or turning the rules into a song that will stick in kids' heads.

Just try not to overload them or give conflicting instructions, and you will find that kids have a much easier time remembering what's expected of them.

They Are Distracted

Kids have fairly short attention spans. They usually find it difficult to concentrate on tasks that don't interest them, and they may have trouble paying attention to directions if there are a lot of other things going on at the same time. You've probably seen for yourself just how short your kid's attention span can be. You've just gotten them settled with some crayons and paper, you leave the room for half a second, and when you come back they're onto some new activity. This brief attention span can cause difficulty following rules and listening, as there may be some other activity that looks more interesting to them.

Distractibility is only amplified by modern technology and toys. If you're trying to talk to your child but they're watching a TV show, playing a video game, or messing with a toy while you're speaking, they're not giving you their full attention. This means they're more likely to ignore what you're saying in favor of the fun toy or game.

There are a few solutions you can try for this. One is to make sure you have their kid's attention by asking them to pause their game and listen. Only ask them to do something when you know they're actually paying attention to what you're saying. Another method is to make the activity you want them to do fun so they naturally want to listen. If you turn clean-up time into a game or contest, your child is more likely to give it their attention instead of getting distracted by more fun tasks.

We Are Distracted

We can be just as distracted as our kids sometimes. As parents, we have to juggle a lot of tasks and responsibilities at the same time. In the morning alone, we might have to worry about breakfast and packing lunches, getting the kids up and ready for school, and getting ourselves ready for our days all at the same time, and our to-do list may only get more crowded from there. With so many thoughts running through our heads and so many tasks we need to do each day, it's hard not to be distracted when we're talking to our kids. But distraction gets in the way of good communication. It keeps us from paying attention to what we're saying and how we're saying it, which can lead to miscommunication and sometimes hurt feelings if we say or do something without thinking about the consequences.

To get the best response from your child, make sure you are giving them the same attention they are giving you. Try not to yell instructions across the house. If you can, pause what you're doing and make sure your child is looking at you before asking them to do anything.

We Are Using Harsh Language

The language we use when we're talking is often more important than what we're trying to say. If we're trying to tell someone they're doing a task incorrectly, they're more likely to listen to us if we gently correct them rather than criticizing the way they're currently doing the task. We tend to soften our tone when we're talking to other adults, but we can sometimes forget this when we're talking to our kids. Of course, it's equally important to pay attention to the language we use in both situations.

Kids may be more resistant to what we're telling them if our words feel like criticism or if we make them feel foolish for doing it wrong. If our first impulse is to laugh or mock, we should pause and consider our words more carefully. If your child is doing something incorrectly, instead of saying "you're wrong," try saying "this way is better." Your child is less likely to get defensive and upset, and more likely to try out the new, better method.

We Are Too Passive or Too Assertive

The most effective form of communication is the middle ground between passive and assertive. If we command our kids to do something, they might resist just because they feel we're being unfair. Making many demands or promising strict punishment if our kids don't comply can make them resent us over time. On the other hand, pleading with our kids to follow the rules undermines our authority. Either option will result in kids who learn not to listen to directions.

Strike a balance between these two extremes. Remain firm when you ask your child to do something, but avoid outright ordering them to do it. Don't cave to your child's desire or lack of desire to follow your rules, but don't immediately escalate the situation to something more aggressive when it doesn't need to be so confrontational. As an example, let's say you want your child to finish their homework. If you say "Finish your work or else!" they'll feel bullied into listening, but if you say "Could you please, please work on your homework?" your child might feel like they don't need to follow your instructions. Instead, try something like, "It's time to work on your homework." This provides direction without leaving room for unreasonable arguments, and at the same time doesn't feel quite as commanding. You can also try explaining why getting their homework done is important so they'll feel more compelled to complete it on their own in the future.

We Don't Follow Through

If our kids ignore us, we need to show them we are serious about our rules. This means following our words with actions. If you ask your child to follow an instruction and they continue to refuse, follow through with an appropriate punishment. If they won't pick up their toys, let them know they won't be getting one of their toys back until they clean up. If they aren't listening to you, a time out may be an appropriate punishment.

One important thing to keep in mind when deciding on consequences for your child's actions is to avoid lashing out in anger. You might be so worked up about your child's behavior that your immediate reaction is to yell, hit, or exaggerate the punishment in comparison to the offense. However, these are not appropriate punishments, and they don't help your child learn to behave. Punishments given out of anger are typically too harsh and often scare kids rather than teach them. If you feel yourself getting upset, take a moment to calm down before you decide on a consequence.

EXERCISES FOR ENCOURAGING KIDS TO LISTEN

Invite your child to take an active role in developing their own listening skills. Changing the way you interact with your child is only half of the solution to bad behavior. The other half is getting your child to practice their listening skills and their own ability to communicate. You can accomplish this by engaging them in exercises that encourage their participation and development. Try out some of these approaches with your child and take notice of how they help you improve your communication with each other.

Speak Face-to-Face

Our faces are incredibly expressive. If someone speaks to us with their face turned away, it's harder to know how they feel. We can listen to the tone of their voice, but we miss out on a lot if we can't make that face-to-face connection.

When we talk to our kids, we should try to make the same connection. This means looking at each other while talking and getting down to their level. We want to eliminate any barriers that could be making communication more difficult, and this is a great way to do it. When we look our kids in the eyes and encourage them to do the same, we make sure everyone is giving the conversation their full attention. We also teach our kids to respectfully listen when someone's talking.

Listen to Your Child

If we want our kids to be good communicators, we have to show them how to listen. Practice giving your child your attention and taking an interest in what they have to say. When we showcase these good practices, our kids will subconsciously replicate them. They'll understand how to be good listeners when they see you setting a good example.

On top of being a good role model, listening can help you understand how kids process events. You'll learn more about who your child is and where they might be experiencing difficulties with their ability to communicate. For example, you might notice that certain topics seem to halt communication. Maybe your child is all too excited to tell you about what they did during recess, but they clam up when you ask about what they learned in class. This might suggest they're having trouble in one of their classes. Other times, you might pick up on your child's difficulties expressing certain emotions. They may have trouble putting their fear or anger into words, which you might not have noticed if you hadn't made the effort to listen more carefully. Once you know where the difficulties are, you can take steps to fix them, whether that means looking into tutoring options or helping them label their feelings.

Figure Out What's Causing Conflict

Disobedience is rarely the result of stubbornness alone. Kids who don't tend to listen to their parents often have stress in their lives that could be contributing to the issue, or there may be something holding them back from completing certain tasks. If you never ask your child why they don't want to do what you ask, you might miss out on a chance to directly address the underlying issue.

Speak to your child and try to figure out why they're not following instructions. Maybe there's something they don't understand about the task you've given them, or maybe they don't understand why the task is necessary. Clearing up these issues means that next time you want them to do the same task, you'll face less resistance.

Keep Your Cool

As we previously discussed, losing our cool can make it a lot harder to get our kids to listen to us. If they feel like they're being unfairly yelled at, they'll be less inclined to see why the task or rule is necessary. If you feel yourself getting angry when your child isn't listening, breathe deeply and stay calm. Avoid shouting at your child, as this can make them even more uncooperative. Use a calm but firm tone of voice when you speak to them, and treat them as you would want to be treated in return.

Explain Why They're Not Being Respectful

Kids may be disrespectful without realizing the harm it causes. When they choose to ignore you, they might not notice how it makes you feel. They also may not have a good grasp on what's considered polite and respectful behavior yet. Sit them down and explain to them that ignoring someone when they're talking is hurtful. Talk about how it's frustrating when they don't listen. Don't be afraid to show emotional vulnerability. Talking about your feelings can encourage them to open up about their own.

If your child is still having a tough time understanding why what they're doing is wrong, you can try turning the tables with a short exercise. Let your child know ahead of time that for about 10 minutes, you won't be listening to anything they say. Make sure your child understands that this is just an exercise to show them how you feel when they don't listen to you. By the time the 10 minutes are up, your child will understand that it hurts to be ignored. (Obviously, don't do anything that might seriously frighten or upset the child.) They will know how you feel when they choose to ignore you, and they will think twice about ignoring you in the future.

Make Listening Fun

Sometimes kids ignore us because there's something more fun they'd like to do instead. If you feel like you're constantly battling for your child's attention, try making the task you want them to do equally or more fun than what they're doing. If you want them to clean up their room, try timing it and letting them see how quickly they can put their toys away. If you'd like them to do their chores, make a chore chart and reward them when they've successfully completed their chores for a certain number of days in a row. This gives your child an incentive to listen to you and cooperate with you. When they see these tasks as fun, they'll often complete them without any complaints.

Don't Expect Overnight Results

Finally, give your child the time they need to adjust to new rules and develop listening skills. Your child isn't going to go from ignoring you to listening to every word you say overnight. Kids need enough time to get used to these new ideas and rules—especially when they are larger in scope—before they can put them into practice. Be patient with your child and work with them if they start to fall back into old habits. If you gradually introduce them to tasks and activities that will improve their listening skills, they're more likely to adopt permanent good listening habits. This will be more beneficial in the long run for their communication skills.

5

START DOING THIS AND WATCH WHAT HAPPENS IN 7 DAYS !

I n this chapter, we'll take a look at some of the best methods for improving communication with your child. You'll learn about different exercises and activities you can use to encourage your child to better understand their emotions, understand how to handle strong emotions, and calm themselves when they're upset. You'll also learn about different tips to get your child to speak more frequently and more honestly about any difficulties they may be facing and might need help with. This chapter also includes methods for improving your own communication skills for talking with kids based on the information you have learned thus far about child development. These exercises will improve communication between you and your child, ultimately leading to fewer arguments and a deeper parent-child bond.

Each of these methods have been proven to improve communication with young kids. They are strategies and techniques that have consistently led to significant results and, in some cases, have been the catalyst for a more positive and genuine parent-child relationship. However, while each of these methods are worth trying, it's important to keep in mind that not every method will work for every child. Some kids may not respond as well to a strategy as others, and that's okay. Every child is unique, and it's alright if you go through a few different strategies before you find what works for you. Be patient, repeat the methods as necessary, and pay attention to how your child responds to each new strategy you try. If you notice an improvement in listening and communicating skills, you're on the right track. If they're still having difficulty paying attention and following your directions, try another one of these tips. While this trial-and-error process can be a little frustrating at times, it is necessary to ensure you are using the best strategies.

METHODS FOR IMPROVING COMMUNICATION

The way we approach teaching our kids better communication skills directly impacts how good at communication they will be. We are role models for our kids, and while they will learn a lot from their teachers, other guardians, and peers, most emotional education occurs inside the home. If we set a good example for our kids and we give them the tools they need to be good communicators, they will have an easier time excelling in other areas of their lives.

The following methods are specifically tailored to teach our kids everything they need to know to form and maintain healthy relationships. When they learn to listen carefully, weigh their responses, and articulate their feelings, they will have more success in conversations with adults and other kids alike. They will be able to understand and explain their emotions to others without confrontation, and accept our gentle correction of the way they choose to express their emotions, which leads to better solutions without tears. They will listen better not because they are afraid to ignore us, but because they want to make us happy and proud—and because we want to do the same for them.

Talk During Downtime

Previously, we have discussed the importance of making sure you have your child's full attention when you're asking them to do something. While this is important when we want to be sure they're listening to us, these aren't the only kinds of conversations we want to have with our kids. We also want to be open and honest with them, and able to speak comfortably about a wide variety of topics. We can speak to our kids no matter what we're doing, whether we're in the car, at the store, or just relaxing around the house.

If you have some downtime when neither you nor your child is doing much more than busywork, fill the gaps with conversation. Talk to them while you're making dinner or driving them home from school. Ask them about their day, and talk about anything fun or interesting that happened during yours. Invite them to give their opinions on different topics, including arbitrary things like how they enjoyed their lunch or what their favorite movie is and why. The simple act of encouraging more frequent conversation can greatly improve your relationship with your child as you start to learn more about who they are and what they enjoy. You should be able to talk to your child as comfortably as you would a good friend. Show a genuine interest in getting to know them and they'll want to talk to you too.

Create Talking Rituals

We all have times when we're receptive to conversation. If you wake up groggy in the morning and haven't had your coffee yet, you might only give short, terse answers to any questions you're asked. If you're exhausted after work, it's possible that the last thing you want to do is answer a flurry of questions, but it's also possible that you'd prefer the opportunity to vent about the tough parts of your day. You might also get annoyed if you feel like you're getting interrupted in the middle of your story with too many questions, or if someone doesn't show enough interest in what you're saying. Conversation style preferences can vary from person to person, and maintaining a good relationship typically involves adapting to the other person's style of talking.

Our kids also have conversational preferences. They may be more open to talking after school, or they might be especially chatty in the mornings. They might enjoy being asked about their day, or they might prefer to guide the topic of conversation themselves so they can talk about what they enjoy and avoid the things that made them frustrated. Picking up on their preferences can help you have more beneficial conversations with less arguing. In particular, get a feeling for when your child is most chatty and how involved they'd like you to be in the conversation. Some kids are content to ramble with less input from you, while others need coaxing to feel reassured that you care about what they have to say. If you keep interrupting a rambling child to ask about small details, you might frustrate them. If you don't respond to a child who needs a bit more prompting to speak, they might get discouraged and trail off. Either misstep can halt the conversation in its tracks and make kids more resistant to listening in the future.

Identifying and adapting to these preferences can help you avoid the hidden landmines that can derail conversations and lead to hurt feelings and frustration.

Be Genuine

Parents often want to make sure they're responding to their kids in the "right" way. To this end, we will often adjust our natural responses to sound more encouraging or less negative. For example, if our child says they weren't asked to play at lunch by their friend, we might immediately jump to saying "That's horrible! They should be ashamed. I'm calling the teacher right now," even if this interference and intrusion in our child's personal life is more detrimental than it is helpful. On the other hand, we might play down our response with a simple "Oh, that's sad," which can make our child feel like we're not listening to their concerns.

We want to know what the best reaction is to anything our children tells us, and we often worry that saying the wrong thing could hamper communication. While saying cruel or uncaring things would certainly get in the way of healthy communication, often the best advice is the same given in almost any social situation: be yourself. You only need to be honest and genuine in your responses.

Exaggerating or understating your responses can make conversations feel stilted and awkward. When you do this, you're not trying to connect; you're trying to analyze your child and come up with the best response. This is exhausting and unnecessary. Your child isn't your boss. While you do need to pay attention to what you say, you don't have to carefully curate your response out of fear of being fired or other consequences. Speak your mind when your child talks to you, as this tells them you're interested in what they're saying. This way, they'll want to share more.

Pay Attention to Details

When we tell a story, we want to know that the other person is listening. If we spend a long time talking about everything we did on our last vacation, it's frustrating to talk to the same person a few days later and have them ask if we saw a certain landmark. We know that while they were ostensibly giving us their attention, they weren't really paying close attention to what we were saying. Maybe they were distracted by something they were doing or had other things on their mind, but it can still make us feel hurt because we know they didn't really listen to us.

Our kids want to know we're listening to them too. If they start to tell a story, try to follow along as closely as you can. Kids' stories can sometimes be told in a complex, somewhat scattered way, but if we really pay attention we can usually get a better picture of what our kids are trying to tell us. Paying attention to the details can also help us uncover details that our kids didn't mention. For example, if we notice they said they were playing with someone as recess who they don't usually mention, we might ask why that is. They might say they made a new friend, or they might reveal that they're in an argument with their usual playmate. This is important information that we would have missed out on if we didn't listen to the details of their story and ask questions.

Use "Door Opener" Statements

"Door opener" statements are simple words and phrases that show your conversation partner that you're interested in what they're saying. These phrases are meant to "open the door" to continued conversation, inviting the other person to step inside and keep talking. They're easy ways to ask for more information, react to what you're being told, and respect the other person's time and opinions. Door opener statements include phrases like "That's interesting," "Really?" and even a simple "Uh-huh" or "M-hm" in between sentences. While these phrases don't really add much to the conversation from an informational standpoint, they can help facilitate conversation by showing your child you're paying attention. They also encourage you to keep your mind on the conversation, as you have to respond rather than just passively taking in information.

Door opener statements are an important part of active listening. When we listen passively to someone else, we don't contribute to the conversation. When we're active listeners, we may speak back and forth with someone else, or we might find another less verbal or non-verbal way to get involved.

To understand the idea better, imagine a classroom. If the teacher stands at the board and lectures for an hour, the kids are listening passively. They might start out interested, but after a while that interest might fade away as they get distracted or disinterested. They might start doodling in their notebooks or daydreaming about playing outside, since they're no longer part of the conversation. On the other hand, if the teacher invites their class to answer questions, ask questions of their own when they don't understand something, and take notes, this encourages active listening. Kids pay more attention when they feel like they're part of the conversation, and so do adults. Even waiting for the right time to add an "M-hm" keeps our brains focused on what the other person is saying. Active listening can also involve making eye contact and nodding or shaking our heads. When we listen actively, we're more likely to pay attention and retain the information.

Sprinkling some door opener statements into a conversation can help us keep our focus on the other person and ensure that when it's our turn to talk, we're ready to participate.

Use More 'Dos' Than 'Don'ts'

It's a lot easier to know what you don't want your child to do than what you want them to do. You know you don't want your child to argue with you, make a mess, or act disrespectfully toward other family members or teachers.

Because of this, it's easy to make rules about what behaviors we want them to avoid. However, it can be a little harder to identify what we'd like our kids to do instead. Telling our kids what not to do can make them feel restricted by rules without giving them clear directions about what is acceptable behavior. When kids only know what not to do and not what they should be doing, they're more likely to break rules because they don't have anywhere to direct their energy.

Instead of coming up with a list of 'don'ts,' try to give your kids instructions on what behavior is expected of them. If one of your rules is "don't watch TV an hour before bedtime," you can revise it to say "start winding down an hour before bedtime." You might give them calming activities like reading or coloring to keep them occupied without making them hyper before they need to go to bed. If you would normally tell your child "don't leave your toys out around the house," try telling them to pick up after themselves when they're done playing. Instead of "don't yell," you can say "speak softly," and instead of "don't hit," you can say "take deep breaths when you're mad and keep your hands to yourself." The action you want them to take is the same, but the way you ask makes all the difference. It gives your child a way to comply without their feeling reprimanded. Using 'dos' instead of 'don'ts' also helps kids feel like they're doing the right thing. They feel good about themselves for doing what you want and you can praise them for good behavior, which is something that is harder to do if they're only told not to do something.

Talk With Your Child, Not at Them

A conversation requires two active participants. If one person is talking "at" the other, not allowing them to get a word in edgewise and disregarding their opinions, this is a lecture, not a conversation. It's important to invite your child to talk with you rather than simply talking at them. Ask them to be part of the conversation too. If you talk "at" your child, you might look outside at a stormy sky and say, "put your raincoat on." Your child might resist simply because they feel like they don't have a choice. Instead of having a one-sided conversation, you could say, "Look at the sky. What do you think the weather is going to be? If it rains, how are you going to keep yourself dry?" This involves them in the decision, rather than separating them from it. .

Talking with our kids reinforces the idea that their opinions are valuable and allows them to express some agency. If we disregard this and talk at a child, we give the message that their thoughts and feelings are not important or interesting, and that the parenting relationship is about the child doing what *you* want" (van der Linden, n.d., para. 16). Ideally, the relationship should be about the two of you supporting the growth and development of your child.

Kids should be able to give input when appropriate, and they should know why they have to act a certain way if it's a non-negotiable issue. When you sit down and talk to and with your child rather than at them, you show them you want them to understand not just what the rules are but why they're important. You invite them to give feedback about which rules are difficult for them to follow and why that might be the case so you can address any problems they might be having, resulting in better behavior and communication.

Use 'I' Statements

Kids need to understand how their actions and words impact the people around them. They tend to take a self-centered view, in part because they are still developing the parts of their minds that allow them to see things from someone else's point of view. We can help them get into the habit of considering the consequences of their actions by using 'I' statements. These are statements that show things from our first-person perspective and help us communicate our feelings or thoughts.

The most common type of 'I' statement is the "I feel" statement. This helps us explain our emotions in a non-confrontational way. If our kids are constantly demanding our attention when we're tired or distracted, we might say, "You're being annoying." This can make kids feel upset, especially if they didn't realize the effect their actions were having on us. Instead, we can say, "I feel too tired to play with you right now," or "I feel frustrated when you don't listen to me." If our kids say something mean to us when we discipline them—something intentionally hurtful like "I hate you"—we can resist the urge to respond with something we might regret and instead say, "I feel upset when you talk to me that way." This is a more neutral way to state the problem that still helps kids recognize the role they play. Our kids will then feel more inclined to change their behaviors because they understand the way these behaviors are hurting us.

There are other kinds of 'I' statements that can help you get your point across. With 'I' statements, "Your room is messy" becomes "I would like you to clean your room." "Stop crying" becomes "I need you to calm down and talk to me so I can understand what the problem is." Often, 'I' statements are what we really mean to say in these situations once we calm down and discard our immediate emotional response. They are more productive for problem solving and they encourage kids to start considering how their actions make others feel. This is a skill that every child needs to learn at some point in their lives in order to have healthy social relationships.

Make Your Requests Important

While it's important to show our kids the same respect we'd like to be shown, we also have to remember that ultimately, we're the ones in charge. If we are too passive in our requests, we risk being ignored. This can make us frustrated and lead to us lashing out at our kids. When we ask them to do something, we need to let them know that we expect them to do it. If we use passive language like "Could you please take off your shoes when you've been out in the mud" or "Would you like to wash your hands before dinner?" we are more likely to be ignored or rejected, especially if our kids are already doing an activity that they find more fun than the one we're trying to get them to do.

Be direct with your words, and if your child resists doing the task, give them a reason why it's important they get it done now other than "because I said so." For example, if you want them to help set the dinner table, you might say "please help me set out the plates for dinner. If you do, we can eat soon." Let them know why you want them to act so they can see why agreeing is in their best interest. You are still making a request, but you're not asking a question they can say no to in most circumstances.

As your child gets older, you likely won't need to be as strict in your requests. Once they understand why a given task is important, they will put up less resistance. They may also have responsibilities that keep them from being able to follow your instructions right away. For example, they might have a lot of homework they need to get done, so they can't clean their room as soon as you ask them. If this happens, ask them when they'll be able to do it and hold them to their promise. This compromise shows mutual respect while still telling your child that they need to listen when you ask them to do something.

Use Kind Words

Many parents say mean and judgmental things to their kids, often without thinking through what they're saying. They might tell their kids, "You're acting like a baby," or, "You're being a brat." What they really mean to say is that the kids' behavior is unacceptable, but because the parent used unkind words the message gets muddled. It becomes a personal attack rather than an attempt to get kids to listen and correct their behavior.

These cruel words typically come more from a place of frustration than anything else, and while they might not be meant to be harmful, that doesn't change their hurtful effect. Just imagine if your boss came up to you and started speaking to you in the same tone you use with your child.

Imagine if they constantly criticized you and your efforts, especially if you didn't fully understand what they wanted you to do. You would be upset, angry, and resentful, and it might impact your ability to listen to your boss in the future. You might purposefully do things you know you aren't supposed to in an effort to get back at them. In short, you wouldn't feel very cooperative at all.

Our kids react in much the same way when we are unkind to them. They may also develop issues with their self-image and self-esteem if we repeatedly criticize them. We may not even recognize the harm we're doing until down the road. The best way to avoid this problem is to shift the language we use to talk to our kids. Be more considerate toward your child and accept that they will make some mistakes. Differentiate between bad behaviors they do because they're being malicious and bad behaviors that are accidents, or ones that only occurred because they didn't know any better. If your child breaks something accidentally, this should be treated differently than if they smashed something out of spite. Instead of punishment, practice kindness and forgiveness. This teaches kids that it's okay to make mistakes and that they can come to you with problems without fearing they'll be yelled at for an accident. Building this trusting and accepting relationship early on is crucial for navigating the more chaotic teenage years. Let your child know that no matter what they do, you'll always love them, and never resort to name-calling or other harsh criticism.

Make sure to praise kids when they do something well too. If they are playing nicely with another child, let them know they're doing the right thing. If they take the initiative to help with clean-up, be sure to thank them. This reinforces good behaviors, which can be even more powerful than discouraging bad ones. Kids feel good when you praise them, which creates a positive feedback loop that results in better behavior. Again, we want to reward the effort, not necessarily the result. Instead of saying, "I'm proud of you for getting an A on your test," we can say, "I'm proud of all the studying you did." This tells kids that good behavior matters more than any grade ever could, and it also reminds them that you'll love them regardless of how well they do in school. If your child studies hard and gives a test their all only to get a bad grade, they shouldn't have to worry about your reaction. Instead, they can bring you their test grade right away.

PHRASES FOR WHEN KIDS AREN'T LISTENING

When our kids aren't listening to us, our first reaction is typically anger and frustration. At this point, we are arguing, not talking to each other or listening to what the other person has to say. This impedes good behavior and turns an opportunity for education into a cacophony of tears, yelling, and hurt feelings.

If your child is refusing to listen to you, there is a wall standing in the way of good communication. Breaking down this wall is important for reestablishing trust and understanding. However, if we try to forcefully knock the wall down by yelling, pulling, or hitting, we do more harm than good. Instead, we must stay calm, reassess the situation, and redirect our kids so they listen to us again. To accomplish this, we can use different phrases that help dispel tension and better understand each other. If they're ignoring us, we can say, "I feel upset when you don't listen to me." If they are starting to yell, asking them to "lower your volume" is more effective than yelling right back. These phrases can turn an emotionally charged situation into a learning opportunity. It is only through this process of clearing the air, de-escalating the conflict, and bringing kids' attention back to ourselves that we can get kids to communicate with us and listen to us once again.

Use Your Inside Voice

Parents aren't the only ones who are tempted to yell when something's going wrong. Kids can get worked up too, and they might scream or wail if they're not getting their way. This is never a productive way to have a conversation. When a child is yelling, they're not ready to listen. But if we tell kids to "be quiet" or "shut up," we're telling them not to make noise at all. We're silencing them and telling them we don't care what they have to say. This usually isn't something they could do even if they wanted to.

Instead, try telling upset kids who raise their voices, "Use your inside voice." This tells your child a few things. The first is that the current volume of their voice is unacceptable and it needs to change. The second is that you're not going to be able to listen to what they're trying to tell you unless they lower their voices.

Finally, this phrase also tells kids that you do want to hear their point of view. You are interested in what they have to say; you just don't want to hear it at 90 decibels. When you put things this way, kids see lowering their voice as a step toward getting you to listen to rather than ignore them. It becomes something they want to do because they know the outcome will be positive for them, with the added benefit of being positive for you too.

Do You Want Help?

We often try to rush in to help our kids, and fix whatever is wrong right away. If our kids are attempting to tie their shoelaces and getting upset when they can't do it, we might demand they just give the shoe to us so we can finally leave the house. When we do this, we take the agency out of our kids' hands. We tell them they're not good enough to do it themselves, and we take away their ability to improve their motor skills. We risk making them more upset because they see their attempt as ending in failure.

Rather than grabbing the reins right away, try asking your child, "Do you want some help with that?" This puts the ball in their court. They can choose to ask you for help or continue to work at their task and figure it out for themselves. The important thing to remember if you ask your child if they want help is to listen to the answer they give. If they say no and you immediately disregard it, they're not going to feel like they have any control. Let them ask you for help before you take over.

Use Your Teamwork Skills

As your child learns new social skills, help them give a name to these skills. When they play nicely with a sibling or classmate and they take turns being in charge of the game, let them know that these are teamwork skills. When they make an effort to listen quietly and attentively when you're talking to them, praise them for their listening skills. By naming these skills, you encourage your child to keep practicing them. You can also remind your child of these skill sets when they forget to use them.

When you're correcting your child, use positive language. If you notice your child is playing with friends and they're always the one in charge, you might be tempted to tell them no one will want to play with them if they're bossy. This kind of negative language tells your child what they're doing is wrong but doesn't help them fix the problem. It just makes them feel bad about their actions. If you wanted to give this a more positive spin, you might tell them to use their teamwork or listening skills. This reminds them that others might want to decide what game they're playing—without making your child feel bad for the way they acted. It is a gentle encouragement to alter their behavior.

The type of skills you suggest depends on the situation. If you need them to settle down and concentrate on one assignment, you might ask them to use their focusing skills. In other scenarios, problem-solving or critical-thinking skills might be more appropriate.

It's Okay to Be Upset

Young kids have trouble compartmentalizing their feelings. A small problem can feel like a colossal issue, even if it can be fixed very easily. As an adult, you know there's no use crying over the small stuff in life, but kids typically don't have this awareness. Something as minor as their favorite show not being on or being asked to wear their red sneakers instead of their blue ones can lead to a total meltdown.

In these cases, we might be tempted to tell kids to stop crying or remind them that the source of their anger or sadness isn't a big deal. Rather than getting kids to stop crying, this usually only makes things worse. When we tell our kids to "get over it," we are invalidating the way they feel. It may not seem like a big deal to us, but to them the issue clearly matters a lot. Additionally, telling kids to ignore their feelings can actually make it harder for them to manage their emotions. They may have trouble recognizing their feelings and may not know how to handle it when they can't keep the feeling at bay any longer. To be more considerate of their feelings and promote healthy emotional growth, we can tell our kids it's okay to be upset when things go wrong. It's not weak to be afraid of something, and crying isn't for babies. These emotions are natural, and no child should be discouraged from feeling them.

That being said, the way kids express their emotions can often leave something to be desired. It's fine for your child to cry when they are hurt or afraid, but it's not okay for them to scream, break things, or hit people. Let your child know that while it's okay to feel sad or angry, it's not okay to express their sadness or anger in destructive ways. You can offer alternative methods for dealing with these feelings, like letting them spend some time alone to calm down, or getting them to take a few deep breaths.

The next time your child starts tearing up about something like their favorite show not being on TV, start off by reminding them that it's okay for them to feel sad or angry if they were expecting one thing but got another. Remember that a change in the TV station's programming is a big deal to your child, even if it doesn't seem like much of an issue to you. If they're being destructive, follow this up by saying it's not okay to act that way just because they're upset.

Finally, redirect that anger and sadness into something more productive. Ask them if they'd like to burn off some steam by going for a walk instead of watching TV, or if they'd rather have some alone time.

Put It on Your Birthday List

Just about every parent has been there before: you're in the store trying to buy only what's necessary, and your child races to grab some toy or game off the shelf. You don't want to add an unnecessary surprise purchase to your bill, especially if you're tight on cash this week, but you also know the meltdown that's coming if you say no. What should you do?

The best solution here is usually one that involves delayed gratification. This is the idea that when we wait for something good to happen and we feel like we've worked for it rather than accepting something that was just handed to us, we enjoy it more. Delayed gratification is also a good way for kids to practice self-control. You can tell your child that you can't get the toy or game right now, but if they behave themselves maybe you can get it for them for their birthday, or another closer holiday. Ask them to write it down on their birthday list, or write the list for them if they're too young to do it themselves. When their birthday comes around, they can pick toys they still want to get. This keeps you from buying toys your child will get tired of within a week, and it also encourages your child to be on their best behavior so they can get their reward. When they unwrap their toy, they'll know they got it because of their good communication and listening skills, not because they threw a tantrum in the middle of the store when you said no.

Let's Try That Again

Kids may need to try things a few times before they get it right. This is true for most skills they learn like reading, writing, and dressing themselves, but it's also true for social situations. Maybe you planned a fun trip for the family, but arguments broke out. Maybe your child was trying to show you something they learned but they didn't get it right and they got upset instead. Maybe you tried to deal with your child's fussing and you ended up handling it the wrong way. In these situations, the best thing you can do is suggest a do-over.

If a fun activity or a conversation goes the wrong way, try starting over again. Take it from the top, but this time remember to keep calm and avoid the mistakes of last time. Adjust how you handle a tricky situation so everyone has more fun this time around. Let your child make a few attempts until they have a better handle on their words or actions. A second chance gives everyone the opportunity to recognize how things went wrong before and make sure they don't go wrong in the same way again.

Let's say you wanted to have a family trip to the park, but before you even got out the door you got in an argument with your child. Maybe they started arguing with you about what outfit they wanted to wear. If you don't patch things up, the argument can sour the whole trip. Give everyone a moment to calm down, then ask your child if they'd like to try that again. This time, when you start getting them dressed, try to be more receptive to their opinions and remain calm when you explain why they can't wear a heavy outfit when it's very hot outside. Maybe take them outside so they can feel the temperature for themselves, which will help them realize why your instructions make sense. This is the same scenario again, but this time without all the arguing and hurt feelings. Now you're starting the trip on a positive note.

What Did You Learn?

Every difficult situation is an opportunity for kids to learn something. There is always some new lesson to learn when we go through hardship. We might learn something about ourselves, about how we should act in certain situations, or about other people. If your child experiences an upsetting situation, turning it into something they can learn from is a great way to make the experience a little more positive in their mind. This can ease some of the sting of the situation. Even though it was hard to experience, it was also a necessary experience that taught them more about themselves and the world around them.

As an example, let's say your child had an argument with their sibling. Instead of handling the argument respectfully, they hit their sibling. Your child will probably get upset if you point out how this behavior is unacceptable. If you send them to time out and they're still angry, try asking them, "Do you know why what you did wasn't okay? What did you learn from this?" The lesson here should be that hitting is wrong, and it's better to use your words during an argument. When you reframe the situation this way, your child understands why they're facing consequences for their actions. They also have an easier time remembering the lesson next time they have the urge to hit someone when they're mad.

What Do You Think You Can Do?

If your child makes a mistake, your first instinct might be to fix the mistake for them. If they upset their sibling or a friend, you might try to smooth over the situation yourself. If they got reprimanded for their behavior at school, you might call up their teacher and direct your anger at them. When we take over situations for our kids, we don't help them as much as we think we do. We take away control of the situation, and we diminish the consequences of their actions.

Instead of fixing things ourselves, we can ask our kids what they think they can do to fix the situation. If they made their sibling cry, ask them what they can do to cheer them up. You can suggest an apology if they have trouble arriving at an answer, but let them decide.

Additionally, use this as a chance to reinforce consequences. If they knocked over their toys to purposefully make a mess, let them know the consequence of their actions is to pick up their toys without your help. This will teach them not to repeat the behavior, as they know they will have to work harder to fix it than if you had cleaned up the toys yourself.

I'm Here to Support You

No matter what our kids do, they will always be our kids. We don't want to rescue our kids from situations created by their bad behavior, but we do want to support them when they try to make things right and fix their mistakes. We can let them know we care and want them to succeed. We can remind them we love them all the time so they never doubt it for a moment, even if they make us very mad. When our kids know we're in their corner, they're more likely to listen to us and come to us for guidance with their problems.

As you continue to reinforce good behaviors and discourage bad ones in non-confrontational ways, your child will learn everything they need to know to have a healthy relationship with you and other people in their lives. By encouraging communication and responsiveness, you do so much more than just talk. You are laying the foundation for their future development.

THE ONE VITAL SKILL YOUR KIDS MIGHT BE STRUGGLING WITH AND HOW TO FIX IT !

Of the many skills kids learn when they are still developing, communication is perhaps the most important. Without good communication skills, kids can have trouble relating to their peers. They may struggle to form significant relationships both inside and outside the family. They may argue with you more often, and they can engage in more bad behavior because they don't know any other way to make themselves heard. They see all attention as good attention, even if it means they have to draw attention to themselves by being loud, rude, or disobedient. It's possible they will find it harder to learn when they're at school, as "a child who is good at communicating verbally will find it easier to produce written communications, and thus will likely perform better in their school exams and written assignments" (Kumon, 2016, para. 8).

Despite this, many kids struggle to communicate their desires effectively, simply because they haven't been taught the right way to talk to others. They may struggle to explain how they feel in productive ways, or they may be held back by extreme shyness that prevents them from making friends. If these issues are not corrected in early childhood, they can pose problems for many years. Some communication issues can even follow kids into their teenage, young adult, and adult years. Shyness can develop into anxiety, a commanding or bossy personality can drive away potential friends and impede their social development, and trouble with school could hurt their ability to get into a good college and secure a job. These issues are very far into the future, of course, so you still have plenty of time to make sure your child has the skills they need to avoid them when they grow up. Right now, you can have the greatest impact on your child's future success by teaching them good communication skills.

WHY KIDS STRUGGLE WITH EFFECTIVE COMMUNICATION

Difficulties with communication can make themselves known in a few different ways. Kids who struggle to communicate effectively often try to make their feelings and opinions known another way, mainly through making a fuss and throwing temper tantrums. They don't know how to talk about their wants and needs with their words, so they resort to drawing attention to themselves and demanding what they want. A child who exhibits these behaviors may only be doing so because they don't have the tools for more rational self-expression.

On the other hand, some kids may be too timid to reach out and socialize with people they're unfamiliar with. They might come alive in the home, but as soon as they leave the house, they completely clam up. You might not consider this shyness to be a big deal at first—after all, it's less disruptive than kids who run around and shriek at the top of their lungs in public places—but it can be an indicator that your child is having difficulties communicating. They may have experience being misheard or misunderstood by others, so they have stopped making attempts to communicate. They may be frightened of strangers, or they may have difficulty being honest and open with people when they speak. Any of these issues could point to difficulties with communication.

As much as we might like one clear reason for communication issues, the real answer to why our kids might have trouble communicating effectively isn't so cut and dried. It may be a combination of reasons, each stemming from a social or developmental source. Previous experiences can contribute to how a child expresses themselves. Sometimes, kids just need a little more time to figure themselves out and get their mood swings under control. However, if these issues persist long past when kids should have grown out of them, it's time to take a closer look at your child's behavior. Consider the different factors that could be contributing to their communication difficulties and try to identify whether each one of the following potential sources applies to your child.

A Lack of Guidance

Parenting in the modern world can be very difficult because of how busy we are all the time. Most households can't afford to have one parent stay home with their child all day, which means other childcare solutions become necessary. A child could end up spending more time at daycare, where they are one face among a dozen or more kids, than they do with their parents at home. When we get home from work, we may be so tired that we struggle to give our kids the attention they need for their development. We're more likely to sit them down in front of the TV or let them play on a phone or tablet than we are to still have the energy required for spending quality time with our kids. This parenting style and the increased amount of time kids spend in front of a screen can contribute to difficulties forming human connections. If kids don't get enough practice talking with us, their communication skills can suffer.

Similar issues can arise if we unknowingly set a bad example for our kids. If we argue with our spouse and raise our voices, our kids may overhear this and learn that this is how adults talk to each other. They may come to believe that this is the way they should communicate too, even if we tell them otherwise. Kids learn by seeing, and if all they see are bad examples they will pick up and internalize this behavior.

We can alleviate some of these difficulties by making sure we carve out a little time each day to spend with our kids. This might be during mealtimes, bathtimes, or before bed if we have a busy schedule. Additionally, any time we get to spend with our kids should be spent paying attention to them. If we get distracted with the television or with our phone, we're not giving our kids the attention and feedback they need to develop their social skills.

Trouble With Social Cues

Some kids may have trouble communicating because they don't know how to pick up on social cues. These are the small facial movements and posture changes that tip us off to how other people feel without needing to hear them say it out loud. Kids who aren't great communicators may have trouble "reading a room." They might tell a joke at an inappropriate time, interrupt their conversation partners, or keep a conversation going long after it's clear the other person wants it to end. The social cues that give us this information are recognized so automatically by our brains that we hardly have to think about them, but some kids may not be as adept at picking up these cues as most adults. They can unknowingly make conversations unpleasant or make others feel awkward, which might drive potential friends away and limit their opportunities to socialize.

Some kids just aren't as interested in socializing. This isn't necessarily a bad thing but does mean these kids don't get as much practice reading facial cues and body language as their peers. They can fall behind because of a lack of practice, which makes it harder for them to catch back up.

Not Paying Attention

Lots of kids have trouble participating in the typical flow of a conversation because they're not paying attention. Their thoughts may be elsewhere, or they may be so excited by what they want to say that they forget to listen. Kids who are easily distracted and have difficulty listening may be more likely to interrupt in the middle of someone else's sentence, or they may say something that seems like a total non-sequitur to whatever they were saying before. If you find that you frequently have to ask your child what they mean by what they said, this may be a problem with their language skills.

Similar difficulties that can plague easily distracted kids is proper word choice. They can get their vocabulary jumbled up, or they may spend a long time trying to come up with the word they want to use. When they remember it, they blurt it out, regardless of whether the conversation has moved on in the meantime. Without being able to focus on the conversation at hand, overactive thoughts can become a barrier to natural conversation.

Impulsivity and Anxiety

Impulsive behaviors are those that aren't fully thought through before we act on them. If we act impulsively, we might say or do something we don't mean or we might perform these behaviors without considering how they might affect other people. Kids who struggle with acting impulsively might find it difficult to reign in their gut responses to situations. They may say something they don't know is rude but still has the power to hurt someone's feelings. They might speak as soon as they come up with something to say rather than waiting for a pause in the conversation. They might also get angry if they feel they're not being listened to, even if they're not making an effort to listen to others.

Kids who feel anxious are more likely to act impulsively. They may do or say things that make the conversation awkward for both parties. This can discourage them from participating in the conversation and make their worries worse. They might see their conversational faux-pas as a much more serious event than the simple, fixable mistake it was thanks to their anxiety. They may then act on an impulse to retreat from the conversation, which can keep them from getting the necessary practice to overcome their fears. Impulsiveness and anxiety go hand in hand, and they can each make the other one worse if nothing is done to help your child improve their communication skills.

Communication Disorders

On top of the previous reasons, it is also possible that your child may have a communication disorder that is restricting their ability to hold a conversation. They may have a shortened attention span because of attention deficit hyperactivity disorder (ADHD), or they may have a developmental issue that makes it harder for them to process and communicate their feelings. Kids may also have trouble feeling heard if they have a speech impediment, which can make it harder for others to understand them. If you suspect your child has any of these issues, seek out a specialist for a professional diagnosis. Defer to any recommended treatment plan and ask what you can do to help.

Whatever the reason for your child's difficulties getting their point across, understanding where the issue stems from can help you more effectively address it. If you know your child is having trouble picking up on body language cues, you can practice more activities that involve reading body language. If you believe a communication disorder could be holding them back, you can speak to a specialist. Knowing the underlying issue allows you to take more effective steps to address the problem and improve your child's communication skills.

METHODS FOR IMPROVING COMMUNICATION SKILLS

If your child struggles with communicating, there are plenty of opportunities for you to help them improve their skills. No child is destined to be a bad communicator forever. With some assistance from you, any child can learn to improve their social awareness and their ability to engage in conversation. With these activities, exercises, and everyday practices, you can teach your child more about why communication matters and how they can get better.

Encourage Active Listening

Previously, we mentioned the value of practicing active listening with your child. When you listen actively, you take an interest in what they have to say by nodding your head, offering encouragement or interest, and adding to the conversation without interrupting. Now, we'll take a look at how you can encourage your child to model the same behaviors.

Part of encouraging active listening is demonstrating the behavior yourself. Show your child how it's done before you ask them to try it. Then you can explain to them how to listen actively, and they'll understand how good it feels to know the other person is listening. In conversations, gently encourage them to make eye contact and check in every so often to make sure they're listening. Eventually, they will pick up the active listening behaviors.

As always, listening is an integral part of communication. When kids start actively listening, they're more likely to absorb what they are hearing and pick up on social cues. They'll get a feeling for the natural flow of conversation, and because they're listening actively, they'll be able to respond in an appropriate way.

Expand Your Child's Vocabulary

Difficulties in communicating can arise because kids lack the words they need to express themselves. They may work themselves up with no way to explain how they're feeling other than to cry or yell. We can assist our kids by teaching them to explain their feelings and make themselves understood. The larger your child's vocabulary is, the easier it will be for them to express themselves, and the less they will have to rely on more dramatic outbursts.

There are many different ways you can teach your young child new words. One method is to name emotions as your child experiences them. If you can see them getting red in the face and clenching their fists, let them know they're feeling angry. If they start to tear up, name the emotion as sadness or frustration. Assist them in figuring out the right name for whatever they feel.

Reading is another great way to teach your child new words. When you read together, you can explain any unfamiliar words they might come across. Kids who read more develop a larger vocabulary, which often translates to more confidence in their communication skills. They also tend to have an easier time talking about themselves, and they may even find it easier to identify how others are feeling because they learn to empathize with the characters in their books.

Don't be afraid to use words your child might not know in conversations with them. Many parents simplify their language when talking to their kids, but this ensures the kids won't learn anything new from the conversation. Use more complex words as you would when talking to an adult, and let your child know it's okay to ask for clarification. Sometimes kids can figure out meanings from context clues, but other times they will need explanation. Make sure not to judge them for any words they might not know, as this could discourage them from asking for help in the future.

If you hear your child using a word incorrectly, try to gently correct them. You don't want to overcorrect to the point that you're nitpicking or constantly correcting them, but you also don't want to let them continue using the word incorrectly. This could lead to greater confusion in conversations.

Remain patient with your child, and if you don't understand what they're trying to say, ask them what they mean until you have a good idea of the word they intended to use.

Pay Attention to Your Body Language

Just like active listening, it's easier to teach kids about body language when we demonstrate it for them first. When you're speaking to your child, make an effort to ensure your body language matches what you're trying to say. Keep your posture relaxed and open when you're happy. If you're feeling tense and stressed, let your body reflect this too. The more kids see different kinds of body language, the better they'll become at identifying the emotion behind the body language and picking up on cues they would have otherwise missed.

You can also directly teach your child about body language. Take the opportunity to point out different body language in pictures and TV shows you watch together. You can even mention the body language of other kids your child is interacting with. If another child has their arms crossed and they're avoiding eye contact, explain that this might mean they're nervous or uncomfortable. Ask your child about what they think they could do to help them feel more comfortable and what kind of behaviors would be inappropriate for the situation. Eventually, they will be able to determine the best approach without needing your guidance.

Involve Their Imagination

Kids learn a lot from playing pretend. If you want to help them improve their communication skills, trying role playing some situations they might encounter in their lives with them. Pretend you're another child on the playground and let your child pretend they're meeting you for the first time. You can guide them through a conversation that will help them make a new friend, which lets them feel more comfortable when the situation presents itself in real life. The practice kids get from trying things out in a safe, low-stakes environment is incredibly helpful.

It can also be useful to encourage kids to talk about their emotions by creating stories with their toys. If your child is in an argument with one of their friends, they might find it tough to talk about it with you. They might feel more comfortable playing a game where their stuffed animal was having the same trouble with their friend. It is often easier to say their toy is scared and upset than it is for them to use the same labels to describe themselves. As you show your child how the stuffed animal resolves their conflict, he or she learns to apply the same methods to the conflict in their life.

Talk Frequently

The best way to improve communication is through practice. If kids don't talk, they'll find it harder to develop effective communication skills. If they get the practice they need through conversations with you, they'll be able to use the same skills to talk to just about anyone. Take every opportunity to talk to your child about their day, their feelings, and their opinions. Encourage them to open up but don't be afraid to have a casual conversation either. Talk when you're doing an activity together or when you're just spending time with each other around the house. The simple act of talking is powerful. Your child will feel more comfortable communicating, and they will continue improving these invaluable skills.

PHRASES TO ENCOURAGE MEANINGFUL CONVERSATIONS

Just as we looked at phrases we can use when kids aren't listening, we will also look at phrases we can use to get our kids to open up and talk about topics that are important to them. These phrases are deceptively simple. They can often open the floodgates and get your child to really start talking about what interests them.

What Are You Looking Forward To?

Kids' schedules are usually fairly busy. They probably have playdates with friends, extracurricular activities, and family events in their near future. They might even have a birthday party or two to attend.

There is a lot for kids to look forward to. If you know there's something fun coming up for your child, ask them about it. Ask what they're excited about and what they plan to do that day. This is a natural topic of conversation for kids to latch onto because it's inherently interesting to them. This can help coax quiet or gloomy kids out of their shells, as even the shyest child has interests and fun hobbies they would be happy to discuss with you. It also helps you learn a little more about what your child finds fun and what kinds of activities are exciting to them.

What Kind of Superpower Would You Like to Have?

This is a classic question for all ages. If you're looking for a good conversation topic, ask your child what superpower they would most like to have and why. Would they like to soar over crowds, or would they like to rewind time and undo a bad decision? Maybe they'd like to be super strong, or perhaps they're more interested in invisibility. Whatever answer you get, it's sure to be a fun topic, and it can reveal areas your child might like a little extra help in. For example, reading minds might be more appealing if your child thinks it could help them better understand what other people want them to say. This answer might indicate your child is having difficulties with their listening or memory skills, or that they haven't yet mastered some of the social norms for conversations and they tend to talk out of turn. You can then address these issues with practice and other exercises.

When Did You Feel Happiest Today?

All too often, we find ourselves asking kids to talk about tough emotions like anger and sadness. We want them to explain these feelings, but we rarely pay as much attention to more positive feelings. If we focus too heavily on all the negative parts of life, it might even feel like these emotions are the only ones we ever experience.

Flip this on its head and ask your child about when they felt happiest during the day. They'll speak more enthusiastically, and they'll naturally practice gratitude for the good things in their life rather than dwelling on the difficult moments.

7

NOW LET'S MAKE LEARNING FUN!

Improving communication with your child doesn't have to be all work. You can involve some play in your strategy as well. In fact, making learning fun is one of the best ways to engage your child. It captures your child's attention and helps them feel like they're part of the lesson rather than feeling like they're being lectured at. Using exercises and games allows your child to take part in their own education and gives them an opportunity to practice their skills. It also takes some of the pressure off of getting things right. They have time and space to make a mistake or lose their temper without hurting someone's feelings. When an opportunity to use these skills for real comes around, they will be ready to nail it.

GAMES AND ACTIVITIES FOR COMMUNICATION

The exercises included in this chapter help kids practice different aspects of good communication. These include conversation skills, emotional maturity, empathy, being respectful, and taking turns speaking. Kids are encouraged to identify their feelings in different situations, talk about themselves, and listen to what others have to say. These activities are a great addition to any household game night or lesson plan.

Show and Tell

In show and tell, each participant selects an item that is personally valuable to them. When it's their turn, the child will get up in front of the room and show everyone their object. Then they will explain why they picked it and why. Once they're finished presenting, the other participants can ask questions about the item. You can make show and tell extra fun by giving kids a specific theme for their item. For example, one week you might ask everyone to bring a book they enjoy. The next week, you might ask them to bring a drawing they made. This helps keep things interesting and gives kids some guidance on what makes the item important to them.

Show and tell gives kids practice with public speaking, as they're giving a presentation to family or peers. They get to present in a safe environment where there is no one trying to discourage or mock them. Everyone is giving them their attention, which can help them feel heard and valued. Through show and tell, kids learn how to describe an object to another person. They also learn how to tell a story if they share something that happened to them that involved the item they're presenting. When the rest of the group asks questions about their item, they get practice coming up with answers on the spot. Once they're done presenting, they also get to exercise their listening skills by watching others present and asking their own relevant questions.

Telephone

To play telephone, have everyone sit close to each other in a circle. Designate one person, typically the oldest player, to be the start of the telephone. The starter comes up with a word or short phrase. Then they whisper that phrase in the ear of the person sitting next to them. That person whispers what they heard to the next person, and so on until the message reaches the beginning of the telephone again. Starting with the first person, have everyone say aloud what message they think they heard from the last person. While you might assume everyone will say the same thing, there is usually at least one point where someone mishears or speaks too softly for the next person to get the right message, which means there was a small, often silly miscommunication. The game is most fun when played with many people, as the chances increase that the message will get jumbled as it makes its way around the circle.

The telephone game teaches kids about the way a message can be misheard or misunderstood as it moves from person to person. If they whispered the phrase "tiny cat," the person next to them might have heard them say "shiny rat." Even though neither of them were trying to get the message wrong on purpose, the miscommunication still happened.

This teaches kids to be careful with their words and anticipate that sometimes what we hear people say isn't actually what they meant. This can get them to be more forgiving of miscommunications in the future. It can also help them speak clearly so they have a better chance of being understood and avoiding a miscommunication altogether.

Finish the Story

"Finish the story" is a collaborative game for everyone in the family or class to work together to create one complete story. To play, start with a simple, open-ended introduction, such as, "there was a big brown dog who…" Once you start the story, let the next person continue where you left off. Each person should add a line or two to the story, with no one person contributing too much or too little. Once you've gone around the room a few times, you will have created a story that is entirely unique and shared by everyone.

This game teaches kids to cooperate with others. It teaches them collaboration while also letting them showcase their storytelling skills. The game also asks kids to listen to everyone else when they're talking, or they won't know what to do when it's their turn to add to the story. Taking turns is another valuable lesson the game can teach. Instead of telling the entire story themselves, kids must take turns with everyone else and let them contribute. Each of these lessons is integral to good communication.

Playing Pretend

Playing pretend probably isn't something you have to introduce to your child, as kids tend to pick this one up naturally. They want to mimic the behaviors they see other people do, and they want to let their imaginations run wild. When kids play pretend, they act like someone else for a little while. This could mean they pretend to do what you do, or it could mean they imagine what it would be like to be an astronaut, an explorer, or another dream job.

Aside from its benefits for creativity, playing pretend also lets kids improve communication skills. When kids play pretend as a group, they get used to the idea of designating and fulfilling roles as part of a team. For example, in a group of kids who play house, kids typically decide who will be the mommy, the daddy, the brothers and sisters, and other members of the family. Then they act out those roles and relationships with the other kids. They learn that teamwork often means each person does a slightly different role, even though they're all working toward the same goal. Playing pretend is also great for your child's ability to put themselves in someone else's shoes. This is a great exercise that helps them understand and accommodate other peoples' perspectives.

Emotional Charades

In a typical game of charades, players must act out a word or phrase completely nonverbally. They can only pantomime and try to get their message across without talking. Other players will then try to guess what word the person is miming. In emotional charades, all of the phrases being acted out are different emotions.

To play, write down a list of emotions or situations that might cause an emotional reaction. These might include simple emotions like happy and sad, more complex feelings like loneliness and frustration, or emotional situations like losing something important or getting a new toy. Each word or phrase should be on its own piece of paper. Put all the papers in a bowl and have one player draw a paper. They must act out whatever they see.

Emotional charades helps kids pick up on methods of communication other than talking. They connect different facial expressions and body language to their corresponding emotions as they're acting, and they learn to pick up on these nonverbal cues when they're guessing. This can help them gain a better understanding of their feelings. This is especially true if the phrases everyone is acting out are emotional situations. Through charades, kids learn what they should expect to feel in different situations, which can better prepare them to experience these situations in real life.

Simon Says

Simon says is a game where one person is designated as the leader, or "Simon." Simon then asks the other players to perform different simple tasks, but players should only do tasks that are preceded by the phrase "Simon Says." If a player does a task but Simon didn't use the phrase, they are eliminated from the game.

Simon says tests kids' ability to listen and pay attention. Kids will be focused on whoever is chosen to be Simon because they have to listen to whether or not they say "Simon says."

Winning the game involves carefully listening to what someone else is saying. The game also encourages kids to follow instructions, as they need to in order to play. This creates a mental connection between listening to instructions and having fun. The game can even be used to get kids to do simple chores around the house. For example, some of the tasks you say as Simon might include "Simon says put one of your toys in the bin" or "Simon says pick out a snack for your lunchbox." The games are quick and can be played for only a few rounds if you just want to make cleanup time a little more fun.

Twenty Questions

In Twenty Questions, one player mentally chooses an item that is somewhere in the room. Once they've secretly chosen their item, the other players take turns trying to guess which item they chose by asking a series of yes or no questions. The person answering the questions can only say "yes," "no," "maybe," or "sometimes." After the guessers have asked their combined 20 questions, they attempt to figure out what item the first player is thinking about.

Twenty questions teaches kids to observe and describe their surroundings. They identify key traits about the object they select such as its size, shape, and color, all of which might be questions they need to answer. When kids are guessing instead of answering questions, they learn to consider their words carefully, as they need to figure out which item is the right one without using all 20 questions. They ask more insightful, specific questions that are more likely to give them a better idea of what kind of item they should be looking for. They also learn that closed-ended questions, or those that can be answered by a simple "yes" or "no," are not always the most helpful. They understand that responding to questions with brief answers and minimal explanation can be frustrating for the person asking the question, so they're more likely to ask open-ended questions and give more information in their answers next time.

Board Games

There are many board games that improve kids' communication skills. Each of these games can be used to reinforce communication skills. While they may seem like mindless fun, they're actually teaching valuable lessons.

Classics like *Scrabble* let them practice their spelling skills and can expand their vocabulary. Games like *Battleship* or *Clue* require kids to pay attention and listen to other players' answers to have the best chance at winning. *Guess Who* teaches kids to ask specific questions, and to observe and describe different physical attributes. The various activities in *Cranium* encourage players to communicate in a variety of different verbal and nonverbal ways.

Aside from these specific examples, playing games as a family is a great way to bond and improve communication skills. You're using critical-thinking and problem-solving skills to play games, and you're enjoying your shared time with each other. When you play with your child, you reinforce their belief that you care about them and you want them to have fun. They learn that even though you may argue during the game, and even though you may compete against each other, you still care about each other. Games are a great way to promote learning at any age, and they're an invaluable tool for feeling closer to your child.

CONCLUSION

Parenting isn't always an easy job, but it's a rewarding one. The bonds we forge with our kids are strong enough to last a lifetime, especially if we reinforce them with good communication skills. Our kids may frustrate and exhaust us from time to time, but it's important to remember that kids rarely act disobedient out of pure malice. There are many adjustments we can make to our parenting styles and the ways we speak to our kids that can encourage them to be better listeners and communicators.

Throughout this book, you have learned the best strategies, tips, and secrets for effective parenting that encourages kids to listen. First, you learned the basics of child psychology, getting insight into what makes our kids tick and why they may have trouble listening to us. Next, you mentally prepared yourself and discovered how to keep frustration at bay during arguments and tantrums. Then you learned why communication is so important for kids, how listening makes them better communicators, and how you and your child can improve communication skills. Rather than reacting with anger, you now know that taking time to explain the situation to your child in terms they understand is a more productive method of conflict management. You know how to teach emotional intelligence and conversation skills to your child through fun activities and games. With all of this information, you are now ready to be the best parent you can be. Use this information to guide your child through all the hurdles of early development and prepare them for the rest of their life.

Now that you've learned how to improve communication between you and your child, all you need to do is put your newfound knowledge into practice!

Try some of the tips included in this book, keeping in mind the information you've learned about child development and the importance of remaining calm when talking to your child. Use encouraging conversation starters to get a better understanding of their feelings. Encourage them to exercise their listening skills. The more you practice the methods in this book, the stronger your bond with your child will become. You will develop mutual respect for each other, and before long you will become not just parent and child, but good friends.

If you found this book to be helpful in getting your child to listen to you, consider leaving a positive review on Amazon. This helps more parents, guardians, and teachers just like you get the help they need for establishing communication with their kids. Every parent-child relationship deserves the opportunity to flourish, and practicing good communication skills is the best way to ensure that happens for parents everywhere.

REFERENCES

AnnaliseArt. (2019, July 18). *Family in the car*. Pixabay. https://pixabay.com/illustrations/people-in-cars-family-car-4345551/

Arhavisual. (2019, June 4). *Upset child*. Pixabay. https://pixabay.com/vectors/cry-sadness-child-alone-emotions-4250450/

Cdd20. (2020, Jan. 30). *Angry thoughts*. Pixabay. https://pixabay.com/illustrations/caricature-imagination-hand-drawing-4804618/

Cherry, K. (2020, Aug. 16). *Child psychology and development*. Verywell Mind. https://www.verywellmind.com/what-is-child-psychology-2795067

CoxinhaFotos. (2017, Mar. 1). *Disobedient child*. Pixabay. https://pixabay.com/vectors/son-unemployed-parents-nervous-2106231/

GDJ. (2020, July 5). *Brain and heart*. Pixabay. https://pixabay.com/vectors/mindfulness-brain-heart-mind-body-5371476/

Headspace. (n.d.). *The science-backed benefits of meditation*. https://www.headspace.com/science/meditation-benefits

La_Petite_Femme. (2017, Sept. 17). *Elephants with balloons*. Pixabay. https://pixabay.com/illustrations/elephants-balloons-love-heart-2757831/

La_Petite_Femme. (2017, May 23). *Mom hugging her daughter*. Pixabay. https://pixabay.com/illustrations/mother-and-baby-baby-girl-mom-love-2334628/

MoteOo. (2018, Mar. 29). *Mom criticizing daughter*. Pixabay. https://pixabay.com/illustrations/mom-mum-daughter-mother-family-3273202

Shvets, A. (n.d.). *Wash your hands sign*. Pexels. https://www.pexels.com/photo/drawing-of-hands-being-washed-4226600/

Stosny, S., Ph.D. (2015, Aug. 7). *Why parents really get angry at their kids*. Psychology Today. https://www.

psychologytoday.com/intl/blog/anger-in-the-age-entitlement/201508/why-parents-really-get-angry-their-kids

The Communication Trust. (n.d.). *Why communication is important.* https://www.thecommunicationtrust.org.uk/media/2147/all_together_now_-_section_2.pdf

van der Linden, N. (n.d.). *8 psychologist-backed tips for improving communication with kids.* Motherly. https://www.mother.ly/child/8-expert-tips-talk-effectively-kids

RAISING EMOTIONAL INTELLIGENCE IN KIDS

HOW TO GIVE YOUR KIDS THE BEST KICKSTART TO CONQUER LIFE

 My Top 7 Essential Games to Boost Communication Skills In Children

(Make Learning Fun With These Perfect Tools!)

Checklist Includes:

- 7 Essential Games to Aid Child Development.
- Improve Family Bonding
- Encourages creativity and boost's self confidence
- Links to where you an buy these games for lowest prices.

If your're looking for hacks to accelerate your childs development then this is for you ....

Visit the Link Or Scan the QR Code to get this FREE Bonus Checklist

https://tinyurl.com/Sienna-Checklist

INTRODUCTION

"Our emotions need to be as educated as our intellect. It is important to know how to feel, how to respond and how to let life in so that it can touch you."

— ANONYMOUS

Emotional intelligence is perhaps the most reliable measure of how successful someone will be in life. According to studies, a person's level of emotional intelligence accounts for almost 60% of their ability to succeed in their relationships and career regardless of the field they work in, and 90% of top performers are highly emotionally intelligent (Trotta,

2018, para. 10-11). While other factors like a good education and support from family and friends also play a role in determining one's future, the importance of emotional intelligence cannot be understated. Like many things in our lives, the seeds of emotional intelligence are planted during our childhoods.

We all have emotions, but we don't always know how to name or deal with them. This is especially true for young kids, who may not yet have the vocabulary or emotional maturity to identify how they feel. It's all too common for kids to burst into tears at the drop of a hat, throw an angry tantrum when something doesn't go their way, or respond to a new situation with fear instead of curiosity. Kids often have trouble explaining why they're upset, what caused them to feel this way, and what can be done to resolve the issue. This tends to manifest as kids who are 'difficult' and seem to be purposefully evasive or aggravating, even when they're really just confused.

It's tempting to get frustrated and assume your child is reacting this way because they're being fussy, or that they're purposefully trying to aggravate you. The truth is that your child just hasn't developed the skills to put what's wrong into words yet. If you can show them how to understand emotions and express them intelligently, they'll get a handle on these outbursts, and you'll have an easier time resolving whatever issue caused the distress in the first place.

Of course, emotional intelligence is important for everyone to know, not just kids. When you can assess how you're feeling and what made you feel this way, you can keep yourself calm in stressful situations, properly communicate the problem to others, and work toward a solution. When kids don't learn these skills in early childhood and instead continue to express or repress their emotions in unhealthy ways, they create a pattern of behavior that can follow them long into their adult years. However, if you teach your child emotional intelligence, you'll lay the groundwork for fewer tantrums when they're young and less explosive arguments as they get older. The better your child becomes at communicating how they feel, the better they'll be at listening and problem solving too.

Talking to your child about their emotions doesn't have to feel like interrogating an unwilling participant. Kids can learn to open up about their feelings and have a mature, honest discussion, but first, they need to understand how to name their feelings and effectively communicate them. Whether you're a parent, guardian, or educator, helping your child develop emotional intelligence skills will improve not only your relationship with them but also all of your child's current and future relationships.

If the idea of teaching emotional intelligence is new to you, don't worry; you can still learn and pass these skills onto your child, and incorporate them into your own interactions as well. In *Raising Emotional Intelligence in Kids,* you'll discover why emotional intelligence is so critical to good communication and what it means to be emotionally intelligent. You'll also learn how to help your child find their way through the often complex, confusing maze that is their emotions, assisting them in defining, explaining, and resolving their feelings in a healthy way. As your child learns how to talk about their feelings and understand the feelings of others, tantrums will become less common as more efficient communication methods become the norm instead. You'll have fewer fights, and your child will likely find it easier to make and keep friends. Emotional intelligence is a key factor in getting kids to listen, behave, and prepare themselves for the real world. Reading this book gives you all the tools you need to give this gift to your child.

As a personal life coach, philanthropist, and someone who has a long history of working with kids, it's clear to me just how important emotional intelligence is as a skill everyone should learn, starting in their younger years. I have a firsthand understanding of the difficulties that come from kids who haven't yet developed emotional intelligence, as well as the benefits that come from improving your child's understanding of emotions. I have been studying child behavioral psychology for over 10 years, and during this time I've seen that kids who are encouraged to develop emotional maturity early on in their lives greatly improve their chances of being successful, well-adjusted adults. This book is a way to help as many parents as possible to raise their kids in a way that builds and supports healthy child development by meeting their social needs.

Good communication is one of the most important foundational skills every child should know to help them socialize with their parents, guardians, and peers. This is just as true for the contents of this book as it is in my previous parenting book, *SHHHH...Listen!: Practical Parenting Steps to Get Your Kids to Listen That Work! Age 3-8.* In this book, I focused primarily on how to improve listening and communication with your child through a better understanding of child psychology and anger management for both parent and child. Emotional intelligence involves using healthy communication strategies as well. Through assisting your child in understanding and better managing their emotions, you can improve your relationship with your child and reach a deeper level of understanding with each other.

If you're sick of fights, tantrums, and unexplained fits of crying, teaching your child emotional intelligence can be your ticket to a less complicated relationship with them.

This also paves the way for your child's future success later in life, as those who are emotionally attuned develop the charisma they need to excel both professionally and socially. By improving your child's emotional awareness and expression, not only are you giving them an invaluable skill, you're also solidifying your bond with them for years to come.

1

WHAT IS EMOTIONAL INTELLIGENCE?

Despite the clear importance of emotional intelligence during every stage of our lives, it's not an especially well-known term. Our society tends to focus, and therefore prioritize, more traditional methods of measuring intelligence. Kids are asked to memorize information, and they're then graded on how well they retain this information on different tests and quizzes. As adults, intelligence becomes a badge of honor, and we tend to associate successful people with a high intellect. For all the time we spend holding up this view of intelligence that is measured by our cognitive abilities, the value of emotional intelligence tends to fall by the wayside, despite its importance.

Emotional intelligence has less to do with memorizing and recalling various facts. Like cognitive intelligence, it requires critical thinking and problem-solving skills, but these skills are applied to work out the solutions to emotional problems rather than, for example, mathematical ones. Emotional intelligence is a way of measuring someone's ability to express their emotions clearly and appropriately, to understand others' emotions through their behaviors and words, and to associate different triggers and outcomes with certain emotions. Someone who is highly emotionally intelligent can figure out what emotion they're feeling and why they might be feeling that way and then take steps to correct unwanted or excessive emotions without either shutting themselves off or overreacting. They can also pick up on cues from other people that indicate how they might be feeling, and adjust their own behaviors to account for this. An emotionally intelligent person typically has a good idea of how people react when they experience different emotions, and they can use this to predict and accommodate the reactions of others. Emotionally intelligent people tend to be charismatic, compassionate, and understanding, which is part of the reason why they are well-liked and often find success.

Emotional intelligence can also be seen as a measure of how well we can communicate with other people, both in our ability to understand their wants and needs, and to discern and share our own. If we can improve our emotional intelligence, we can avoid many fights and misunderstandings that might otherwise harm our relationships. By being in tune with our feelings, we can more easily navigate the world around us and interact with family, friends, and strangers alike.

Developing emotional intelligence is especially important for kids. When kids are young, they form their first social connections within the family, with educators, and with their peers. A lack of control over their emotions, and an inability to understand their peers' emotions, could harm these early relationships. For example, if your child gets frustrated and throws a tantrum instead of trying to communicate why they're upset, a teacher might start thinking of them as unruly and spend less time trying to connect with them in the classroom. This might also drive their fellow students away, especially if there is aggression involved. If your child doesn't understand social cues that indicate their friend is upset, they might not realize it until they're crying. They may not know how to apologize for pushing too hard and crossing a boundary, which could strain their friendships. On the other hand, if your child learns more about their emotions and the emotions of others, they can connect with their peers and create positive social connections.

While childhood is an especially important stage in developing emotional intelligence, this pursuit shouldn't end there. Becoming more emotionally attuned should be a lifelong goal. Emotional intelligence is just as important for maintaining relationships and good mental health as an adult as it is for a child. As you guide your child through a basic understanding of emotions and the effects they can have on people, you provide them with the foundations of emotional intelligence, which they will ideally continue to build on for the rest of their lives.

FIVE BASIC PARTS OF EMOTIONAL INTELLIGENCE

There are five core components of emotional intelligence. These are self-awareness, self-regulation, motivation, empathy, and social skills (Ohio University, n.d., para. 2-6). Each one represents a different aspect of social relationships or personal assessment, and each of them are important to learn for different situations.

Self-Awareness

It's very common for kids to lack the vocabulary to explain how they're feeling. For young kids, this means learning what basic emotions such as 'sad,' 'angry,' 'excited,' and 'nervous' mean, and what they feel like. Older kids may need an introduction to more complex feelings like 'jealousy,' 'grief,' and 'insecurity.' A child who is self-aware in regard to their feelings should be able to identify and tell you what emotion they're experiencing. They'll also start to understand how their feelings impact others. For example, they might see how when they get mad and start yelling and making a scene, you become frustrated with them or upset in turn.

Help your child identify their emotions so they get the hang of doing it themselves. Teach them what different emotions feel like so they'll know how to describe them when they encounter them. Let's say you ask your child to put their toys away and they begin to cry because they want to keep playing. Ask them how they're feeling—are they sad because they want to keep playing, or angry or worried because of what you're asking them to do instead? You can also share with them how that makes you feel, as their parent or guardian. For example, you might be sad and frustrated when they don't listen to you. From here, you can have more in-depth discussions about why they feel this way and what can be done to soothe them.

Self-Regulation

Many kids throw tantrums when things aren't going their way. They work themselves up until they are irreconcilably upset or completely furious, and they need to expend that energy—often in inappropriate, aggressive ways—before they feel calm again. This isn't a healthy method for managing emotions, and it can develop into more harmful coping mechanisms as these kids grow older.

Kids who are able to self-regulate are more in control of how they display their feelings. While emotions should never be suppressed, there are constructive and destructive ways to express them, and relying on destructive methods too often can make it harder for them to get a handle on their feelings. Self-regulation involves your child recognizing how they feel, controlling how they choose to express that feeling, and understanding the consequences of whatever form of expression they choose. A child who throws tantrums might put more stress on their family or hurt their friends' feelings. They may also receive a time-out or other punishment for inappropriate behaviors. These are important consequences for kids to learn and consider so they can choose to act accordingly. Instead of throwing a tantrum, a child may pause, recognize they might get in trouble and that the tantrum won't get them what they want, and talk about their feelings clearly instead.

Motivation

Emotions can have a significant impact on motivation. If your child is distracted, upset, frustrated, or anxious, they may have more difficulty getting their work done than they would if they were in a happier mood. It's easy to be motivated when there is very little emotional resistance, but it can be much harder if these feelings interfere with their usual motivation levels.

Kids with a good grasp on emotional intelligence typically find it easier to get important work done regardless of these distracting negative feelings. They should be able to complete classwork as instructed and to do chores around the house. For example, if they don't get the snack they wanted with their lunch, more motivated kids will be able to return to their classroom and focus on the next task the teacher assigns them without feeling distracted by their sadness or frustration. It is normal for kids to take breaks and "recharge their batteries" if they're going through a difficult experience, but they must also learn to compartmentalize these emotions from time to time so they don't fall behind on their responsibilities.

Note that not every issue with motivation can be traced back to regular difficulties understanding and processing emotions. Sometimes this may be connected to more serious mental health issues or difficulties in your child's life, or it may be the result of an attention deficit disorder. If you believe your child's lack of motivation may come from one of these sources, speak with a pediatrician about possible diagnosis and treatment options.

Empathy

Empathy is your child's ability to understand how someone else feels and relate it back to their own feelings. Most kids do not develop empathy until they are around two years old, after which point they should begin to pay more attention to the emotions of others. This can be a difficult skill to develop and practice even for some adults, but far from impossible, especially if empathy is encouraged at a young age.

Empathy allows your child to adjust their behaviors to respond to the feelings of others. They can show compassion because they understand what someone else is going through. As an example, let's say your child is playing a game with one of their friends. Their friend is losing the game, and they're visibly frustrated. A child who hasn't yet built up their empathy skills might continue beating them without regard for how they're feeling, or worse, tease them for losing. On the other hand, an empathetic child may allow their friend to win, or try to find another compromise that doesn't lead to tears. By seeing how their friend feels and adjusting their behavior accordingly, your child uses empathy to maintain social relationships.

Social Skills

Social skills are both a component and an important result of developing emotional intelligence. It is hard for kids to create and maintain friendships if they fail to understand others' emotions and regulate their own. As they practice their social skills, managing relationships with peers and authority figures in their lives, they'll strengthen their social connections, which is very important to healthy cognitive development.

Working with others, practicing patience, and having good manners are key social skills for every child to learn. These are foundational requirements for most healthy relationships. Kids who are socially capable often excel in the classroom and have more positive home lives as well, since they are able to listen, communicate, and understand the actions of others. These kids have the social skills needed to see a rowdy child and offer them a toy to play with as a distraction or to approach a lonely child during recess and invite them into their game. They use their socialization skills to forge bonds with others and often make life-long friends as a result.

Each of the five aspects of emotional intelligence is key to socialization and communication. Throughout the rest of the book, we'll go into more detail about how you can teach your child mastery over these skills through various games and conversations.

COGNITIVE VERSUS EMOTIONAL INTELLIGENCE

Cognitive intelligence has traditionally been much higher valued than its emotional equivalent. The modern education system focuses heavily on increasing kids' cognitive capabilities, and it spends very little time helping them develop emotional intelligence skills, primarily because cognitive intelligence is usually seen as the greatest predictor of future success. But how true is this assumption? To find out, we must first examine both kinds of intelligence and their outcomes on child development.

Cognitive intelligence is measured by a child's intelligence quotient (IQ). Usually, IQ is determined through a standardized test. It's a single number that reflects how cognitively capable someone is, testing their mental and academic abilities. Some of the skills tested include reasoning, memory, comprehension, processing speed, and more. Kids may be asked to complete questions about pattern recognition, logical reasoning, visual and spatial awareness, arithmetic, and making analogies, similar to the skills they learn in standard classroom education.

While these skills are certainly important and necessary for many jobs, are they really an accurate representation of a child's capabilities as they've come to be known? IQ tests often split kids into 'average,' 'above average,' and 'below average' categories, and this categorization can discourage kids from putting enough effort into their studies to improve their IQ. On top of this, IQ may not be as important in our daily lives as we're led to believe. Its accuracy in predicting future success is mixed at best. In short, if you're looking for a single standardized test number to determine if your child will have a good life, you're probably not going to find it through the IQ test.

Now, let's consider a more emotional approach to intelligence. The measurement of emotional intelligence is known as the emotional quotient (EQ). This represents a child's social-emotional skills as understood through their ability to be self-aware, self-regulatory, motivated, empathetic, and social. Standardized tests for measuring EQ are less common. Instead, it is more readily understood by observing kids' behaviors and paying attention to how they interact with others.

A child's EQ, though it isn't always treated with the same seriousness as IQ, may be very important for their development. Socialization is critical during our formative years, and poor emotional intelligence can lead to equally poor social skills. Improving kids' EQs, not just their IQs, shows promise as a way to better prepare our kids for navigating the complexities of the adult world.

	IQ	EQ
Abilities	Heightened cognitive abilities, reasoning skills, logical capabilities, memory, comprehension, and processing speed	Motivation, good social skills, awareness of others' feelings, awareness of their own feelings, and control over their own emotions
Qualities	Academic curiosity, low impulsivity, frequently disorganized, and sometimes lacking a large social circle	Compassion and empathy, good work-life balance, charisma, and frequent emotional expression
Identifiers	Good grades in school, rapid understanding of more difficult concepts, good reading and math comprehension, and seeking out knowledge without being prompted	A large or close friend group, good behavior with few outbursts, willingness to help others, self-confidence, and friendliness toward others

Which Is More Important?

Both IQ and EQ may play a role in how successful your child grows up to be. That being said, the role they play may not be equal. Traditional thought would have us give the edge to cognitive intelligence, but some modern psychologists have started suggesting that emotional intelligence plays a far greater role.

One prominent advocate of EQ's superiority is psychologist and author Daniel Goleman. He believes that "emotional intelligence predicts future success in relationships, health and quality of life" (Kadane, 2020, para. 5) far more accurately than a child's IQ score. High EQ is believed to lead to impressive outcomes such as healthier choices, greater motivation and mental clarity, less risk of getting involved in bullying, and easier adaptation when working as part of a team.

Of course, kids still need to develop their cognitive skills. But in this, too, EQ can often be an asset. Kids who have high emotional intelligence often excel and school, with their cognitive intelligence improving as a result of their abstract thinking, reasoning, and language skills. They have an easier time labeling and discussing their emotions with others, and they can work through emotional roadblocks that might interfere with motivation for other kids. They may also find it easier to ask for help when they don't understand a task, which can make a huge difference in how long they struggle with a new skill before mastering it.

While both IQ and EQ are important, emotional intelligence seems to have a greater impact on who your child will grow up to become. The benefits of emotional intelligence are many, and they are worth cultivating in every child to give them the best life possible.

BENEFITS OF EMOTIONAL INTELLIGENCE

As already mentioned, emotional intelligence can impact kids in a number of different ways. On top of more obvious improvements in cognitive abilities, managing the expression of negative emotions, relationship management, and future career success, kids with high EQs also generally have fewer mental health issues thanks to their abilities to understand and talk about their feelings. EQ may even have an impact on the immune system, yielding an improved resistance to illness. These benefits are just those that have been studied as of now; it is possible that with more time and research, a whole host of other advantages will be discovered, and this will become just the tip of the emotional intelligence iceberg.

The Connection Between IQ and EQ

IQ and EQ may seem to be polar opposites at first, but they're actually far more connected than you might think. As previously mentioned, emotional intelligence can assist kids in improving their cognitive abilities, whether in the classroom or in applying these skills to real-world problems. They frequently do better on standardized exams, and their logical reasoning and critical thinking skills often improve as well. There are a number of reasons for this. It may be a product of a willingness to look for more inventive solutions to different problems. The ability to take an empathetic, compassionate approach to an issue and see things from someone else's point of view is ideal for problem-solving. Kids with high EQs also tend to be more motivated and focused when completing their schoolwork, without the burden of being distracted by unresolved emotions. They can better absorb what's in front of them, and they're often more excited to go to school so they can see their friends. Whatever the reason, if you want to assist your child in improving their cognitive skills, you might be better off starting with emotional skills first.

Healthy Relationships

Emotional intelligence is a key factor in efficient communication, which goes hand in hand with healthy relationships. Since kids with high EQs can identify what others are feeling, and they can get a handle on their own feelings without shouting or hitting, they're often excellent at conflict resolution. There may also be fewer fights in general, as these kids are mature enough to talk about something that hurt their feelings rather than suppressing the hurt until they have an outburst. High EQ kids often develop deeper friendships as well, as they broach more serious topics with their friends and have a genuine understanding of each other. They are likely to have few problems talking to new people and maintaining a friend group throughout their early childhoods, and these skills will benefit them later in life when they start pursuing romantic relationships.

Adulthood Success

The early years of kids' lives lay the groundwork for their teenage and adult years. Achieving success as an adult isn't entirely dependent on having a healthy childhood, but this certainly helps kids get a head start. One study published in the *American Journal of Public Health* tracked a group of kids' development for 19 years. The study found that "a child's social and emotional skills in kindergarten may predict lifelong success. Children who were able to share, cooperate, and follow directions at age five were more likely to obtain college degrees and to begin working full-time jobs by age 25" (Morin, 2019, para. 6). As parents and guardians, we always want our kids to be successful and grow up to achieve only the best things in life. Giving them a good foundation of emotional intelligence provides them with the tools they need to excel in life.

Mental Health

Mental health problems like anxiety, depression, and bipolar disorder are closely tied to emotions. Kids who are highly emotionally intelligent may be better able to navigate these emotions and be less at risk for suffering from mental health issues. Those who do experience a mood disorder such as depression at some point in their lives often seek treatment earlier and find more success with it, as they have less difficulty speaking honestly about their emotions. Emotional intelligence does not always prevent these conditions from occurring, but it may make them less likely.

Self-Soothing

When some kids get upset, they continue to work themselves up and make the problem worse. What starts as a small scare from a scraped knee or a brief sadness caused by something their friend said rapidly evolves into a full-on meltdown that catches the attention of everyone in the area. However, emotionally intelligent kids don't typically follow this path. A child who understands their feelings is better able to come to terms with them and calm themselves down before the situation can escalate. This saves you a headache as a parent, and it also benefits your child in the long run. Self-soothing as a child makes it easier to remain calm as an adult, and it may reduce the risk of developing aggression issues and severe phobias as an adult.

Resistance to Physical Illness

While most of the results of emotional intelligence are seen in a child's thoughts and actions, it's possible it can have a physical impact as well. When we're stressed, our immune system weakens. We have a harder time fighting off illness, leaving us vulnerable to colds and other viruses. Emotionally intelligent kids are better at stress management, so their immune systems are able to function properly. Therefore, kids with high EQs may fall ill less frequently than their peers.

THE IMPORTANCE OF DEVELOPING EMOTIONAL INTELLIGENCE DURING EARLY CHILDHOOD

Early childhood is a very volatile period with a lot of change. It's the point at which kids learn language, social interaction, and an ever-expanding understanding of the world around them. Emotional intelligence is just as important for kids to learn during this time. Most kids undergo the majority of their cognitive development during their younger years, as they start to interact with more people on a more frequent basis.

Prior to attending classes, your child's social circle is probably limited to family and a few close friends, or perhaps some neighbors. The vast majority of social interaction a child experiences during these years comes from their immediate family. As kids start to grow up and attend school, they'll meet and begin to bond with their teachers, their fellow students, and other people outside of the family. Each new conversation carries an emotional message, representing a new experience in your child's life that they can learn from. The more conversations they have and social connections they form, the more these messages repeat, eventually forming the very core of your child's emotional abilities and their outlook. If you encourage your child to be more emotionally aware, they'll solidify a positive relationship with their emotions that they'll carry with them for years to come. The earlier kids learn to understand their feelings and the feelings of others, the easier it will be for them to practice these key skills for the rest of their lives.

The Beginnings of Self-Evaluation

Early childhood is also the point at which kids begin to turn their attention inward and evaluate themselves. They begin to make judgments about who they are and what they're capable of. This can be influenced by our expectations of them and how we react when they do something we don't like.

Prior to engaging in self-evaluation, kids form their ideas of themselves based on what the authority figures in their lives say. If they clean up around the house and you tell them they're being very helpful, this contributes to a positive self-image. If they make a mistake on a homework assignment and you tell them they're not good at math, they'll begin to believe this about themselves too, even if they haven't been given the time to improve. Later on, when kids start evaluating themselves, they might develop a positive or negative self-image based on how you guide their development.

According to the child psychologist Erik Erikson, this period of early self-evaluation is known as "autonomy versus shame and doubt." Kids may view themselves as either an autonomous person capable of growth and achievement or their vision may be clouded by guilt and shame, inhibiting a positive view of themselves. As Erikson claims, "Young children who feel autonomous see themselves as good, valuable people who are able to do what is expected of them in a positive way. In contrast, young children who feel ashamed also feel worthless and incapable of doing what is expected of them" (Oswalt, n.d., para. 6). These feelings of doubt can be difficult to overcome as kids get older, so it's important to teach kids emotional intelligence and encourage them to view themselves in a positive light while their minds are still at their most receptive.

Rapid Cognitive Development During Childhood

We learn information at different rates throughout our lives. When we are young, we pick up our native language just by being exposed to it frequently, and it's easy to master a second language when our minds are still malleable. If you've ever tried to learn a foreign language as an adult, you know it's much harder. Our brains undergo more cognitive development and growth during the first three or four years of our lives than they will ever again. During this time, our brains grow to about two-thirds of their full size, and the pathways inside our brain rapidly evolve in complexity. This makes it easy to learn and internalize new information, especially in regard to emotional intelligence.

With so much development going on in such a short period of time, there is plenty for kids to learn. They are always noticing, thinking, processing, reacting, and adapting to their environments and the people around them. Their emotional experiences contribute to the ideas they hold about themselves, others, and the world at large, and these ideas become more difficult to change the longer they are held. Early childhood is the best time to instill emotional intelligence in kids to give them the best chance at success later in their lives.

2

CRACKING THE EMOTION COACH CODE

As a parent, teacher, or other guardian, you have the opportunity to have a profound impact on your child's emotional development. Depending on your actions, you might leave them to struggle with unknown feelings and allow them to express these emotions explosively, or you might guide them toward a healthy relationship with their inner selves. You are the emotion coach for your child. Whatever you teach them will stick with them and affect how they choose to carry themselves long after they've started a family with kids of their own.

Just like kids start to learn how to speak from listening to their parents, so too do they learn emotional intelligence first through observation. Kids are remarkably perceptive, especially when they are young, despite how we tend to think things will go over their heads. Moments from their early childhoods can have a surprisingly significant impact, even if kids can't actually remember these moments when they grow up and their early childhood memories fade. It is incredibly important to start by cultivating emotional awareness in yourself as you begin teaching it to your child.

HOW YOUR EMOTIONAL AWARENESS AFFECTS CHILDHOOD DEVELOPMENT

In my previous book, *SHHHH...Listen!,* we took a look at how our own troubles with frustration and anger can rub off on our kids, subtly encouraging them to react the same way. If we get frustrated and resort to yelling when we don't get our way, our kids will see this, assume it's typical to behave this way, and become more prone to aggressive outbursts themselves. If we take a moment to gather ourselves when we're angry, and we don't take our anger out on our kids, they will learn to replicate this kind of behavior instead.

The same idea applies to all forms of emotional awareness. Kids learn by watching authority figures. They pick up the healthy and unhealthy coping mechanism we use. Let's say your child is being difficult while getting dressed in the morning. You might start yelling and forcing them into their clothes, fed-up with their behavior, but this only results in your child acting similarly aggressive when someone on the playground won't share with them. If we shove our emotions away, allow ourselves to get swept up in our feelings rather than regaining control over ourselves, and ignore how our kids feel in favor of imposing our own will upon them, they'll learn to do the same. If we look for an unhealthy way to keep ourselves calm like excessive drinking or smoking, they may see these vices as viable coping mechanisms as well. By acting as a good role model for our kids, we can show them what emotions look like, how to handle them, and how to respect others' feelings.

Assessing Your Own Emotional Intelligence

In order to teach a lesson, we must first understand it ourselves. This means taking an honest look at how we deal with issues and out-of-control emotions, especially in front of our kids.

Think about how you react when your child does something frustrating. Are you quick to anger? Do you raise your voice? Do you sometimes say things you don't really mean in the heat of the moment, not realizing what kind of impact it might have on your child? Or do you take a moment to calm yourself before reacting? Do you consider what might have driven your child to bad behavior, and how they might be feeling now? Can you keep a level head while still clearly communicating why what they did was wrong? These are important questions, as they reveal a great deal about your parenting approach and how you view emotions.

You might also have difficulty being empathetic when your child is upset, especially when the reason seems trivial. Have you ever told your child to "suck it up" when they were on the verge of tears, or told them not to be sad when something went wrong? While it's natural to want to see your child smiling and happy, it's also natural for everyone to express their emotions, and forcing away tears just to put on a happy face rarely helps kids calm themselves down. You might occasionally find yourself being dismissive of your child's wants and fears, which can subconsciously encourage them to disregard and shove down their feelings. To help your child deal with their emotions in the healthiest possible way, it's important to watch out for moments when your gut instinct is to dismiss your child's feelings. If they're upset because the weather is too cold to play outside, don't roll your eyes and ignore their distress. Instead, understand that this matters to your child and let them know when it will be warm enough again, or help them find fun indoor activities to do in the meantime. By altering your responses and becoming more receptive to seeing things from your child's point of view, you guide them toward a healthy expression of their emotions and greater emotional intelligence.

FOUR TYPES OF PARENTAL RESPONSES

When your child expresses emotional distress, there are a number of different ways you could respond. You might lend a sympathetic ear, try to find a solution for the problem, become upset yourself, or simply roll your eyes and wait for whatever's bothering them to pass. According to clinical psychologists John and Julie Gottman, who believe strongly in the importance of discovering the emotional source of behavioral issues, there are four possible routes for a parent to take when reacting to their kids' emotions. These parenting styles are the dismissing parent, the disapproving parent, the laissez-faire parent, and the emotion coach (Lisitsa, 2012, para. 3-6). Each parental archetype influences childhood development in a different way.

The Dismissing Parent

If you're a dismissing parent, you might find yourself retreating from emotional honesty. You may be used to ignoring and suppressing your own emotions, and as a result, you unknowingly encourage your child to do the same. It's possible you might catch yourself failing to take your child's emotions seriously, and when something upsets them, you may distract or chide them rather than helping them work through the feeling. These methods usually assume that with enough time, all pains fade, often neglecting to acknowledge that failing to properly address difficult moments leaves them unresolved.

The child of a dismissing parent will likely internalize the idea that emotions are something to be feared. They may take anger, tears, and even outward expressions of joy and shove them down inside of themselves, and they can have greater difficulties regulating their emotions when these built-up feelings become too much to contain. Your child may also see their feelings as unnatural and unwanted, which can interfere with their ability to learn proper coping strategies.

The Disapproving Parent

You can recognize your tendencies toward being a disapproving parent if you react to your child's emotions with a more critical response. Rather than just ignoring the problem, you may notice you tend to actively discourage the expression of emotion. This often involves negative judgments, ridicule, and an authoritative parenting style that makes use of strict rules or harsh punishments for bad behavior.

The effects of this parenting style are fairly similar to those of the dismissing parent but to an even greater extent. Kids may have self-esteem issues, trouble getting their feelings under control, or issues expressing emotions at all.

The Laissez-Faire Parent

The laissez-faire parent model is based on the economic policy of the same name, which means to take a "hands-off approach." If you're a laissez-faire parent, you may be far too lenient with your rules, to the extent that you rarely correct your child's behavior at all. You might have trouble offering any sort of guidance for your child as they navigate their way through their feelings, which can make it harder for them to solve emotional problems or even identify what they're feeling.

The kids of laissez-faire parents often have difficulty concentrating. They may be more rambunctious and less likely to follow rules of any kind. Since they have little experience being taught to regulate their emotions and recognize others' emotions, forming friendships becomes a difficult task.

The Emotion Coach

The final type of parent is the emotion coach, and it's the gold standard that all parents should strive for. It's more emotion-positive than the dismissing or disapproving parent, and it offers more guidance than the laissez-faire method. Emotion coaches help their kids work through their feelings rather than leaving them to manage on their own or willing these emotions away. They are present when interacting with their kids, active listeners, and understanding yet firm in their rules. As a result, kids typically develop a healthy relationship with their emotions.

The emotion coach parenting strategy is fairly rare compared to the others, but it's not an impossible feat if you understand the basics. With a little time and practice, any parent can become an emotion coach for their child, no matter which of the other parenting styles you were previously aligned with.

THE FIVE STEPS OF EMOTION COACHING

To learn how to be an emotion coach, you must start with the five basic steps. These steps are intended to help you alter your reactions when your child needs some coaching. They can help you pump the breaks if you find yourself veering into disapproving territory, or remind you to start a conversation with your child even when you'd be more inclined to follow the laissez-faire approach of ignoring the issue. In a sense, they represent a streamlined method for becoming more involved in your child's emotional development. Adopting these simple approaches can make a world of difference in how you impact their EQ.

Pay Attention to Your Child's Emotions

Think of what happens in the immediate moments before you get upset. You might become more withdrawn. You might curl your hands into fists and stick out your chest for a more aggressive response, or hunch your shoulders forward in a more submissive posture. Kids have plenty of these same tells, and they're often easier to spot than they are on most adults. There are usually many different signs that indicate a more severe reaction is coming, but it's easy to miss them in your child if you're not giving the situation your full attention.

Encourage yourself to be more sensitive to how your child feels before they have to "amp up" their display. Look for signs that indicate they might be getting upset or frustrated so you can intervene before they begin crying or yelling. Kids tend to have the loudest outbursts when they feel no one is paying attention to them. If you learn to look for and recognize the signs of distress early, your child won't have to escalate their reaction to get you to acknowledge their feelings.

Use Emotional Expression as an Opportunity to Teach

It can be hard to feel comfortable talking about emotions if it's not something you're used to. If you grew up being encouraged to ignore your feelings, you might look at your child's emotions as more of an inconvenience or burden than anything else. It helps to alter how you think about the situation so you can respond to it more effectively. Instead of dreading emotional displays, consider how discussions about emotions can help you feel closer to your child. Look for teachable moments whenever possible, and use emotions as opportunities to discuss difficult topics and guide your child's development. When you start actively seeking out these moments instead of avoiding them, you can deepen the connection between you and your child by serving as a guiding force during a time of turmoil for them.

Listen to and Validate Your Child's Feelings

Paying more attention to your child can reveal a wealth of information hiding just below the surface. If your child is trying to talk to you about their emotions, give them your full focus. Put down whatever else you're working on and look them in the eye whenever possible. Help them feel like you care and you want them to succeed. If your child is upset but they can't or won't tell you what's wrong, giving them more of your attention could help point you toward a solution as well.

Part of being a good listener is confirming you've heard what the other person has to say. Listen actively, giving both verbal and nonverbal cues to show your interest. This could be as simple as a nod of your head, or as involved as repeating information back to your child after they say it. This shows them you understand what they're experiencing, and that you're going to help them through it.

Assist Your Child in Labeling Their Emotions

Many young kids lack the vocabulary needed to describe their feelings. They may also have trouble figuring out why they react in a certain way. You can assist them in learning what their emotions are called and what they mean. For example, if your child starts crying, you might ask them if they're feeling sad, lonely, or angry. You may also need to help them reach the answer. Spend some time teaching your child about different emotions so they'll know what to expect when these feelings rear their heads.

Help Your Child Problem-Solve With Limits

While emotional expression is natural, you also need to set limits regarding what's acceptable behavior and what's not. It's okay for your child to feel angry, but it's not okay for them to express that anger by hitting you. They need to find appropriate ways to deal with their anger, such as speaking about it or counting to 10 in their heads.

You can assist your child in establishing coping methods for difficult emotions. Help them develop their problem-solving skills so they can look for a solution to their issue without working themselves up over it. Once they stop focusing on the problem and start looking for the solution, the need to yell or hit may fade as their attention is directed elsewhere. You should also help your child create goals and make plans for achieving those goals. This gives them something to work toward, and something to remember when their emotions threaten to overwhelm them.

EXERCISES FOR EMOTION COACHING PRACTICE

Emotion coaching exercises can be very helpful as tools for education. They help you see emotions as opportunities for learning and for bonding with your child. The more frequently you talk to your child about their emotions, even your own, the easier they will find it to understand their feelings and develop a sense of empathy toward others.

If your child is feeling frustrated, upset, and misunderstood, take a moment to talk through these emotions with them. Treat them with the same respect and understanding you'd like to be treated with, and resist the urge to sweep their concerns under the rug, even if the source of their frustration doesn't seem like such a big deal to you. Kids are more likely to get upset about small things because they have experienced much less over the course of their lives. To them, not getting the toy they wanted may very well feel like the end of the world, and telling them it doesn't matter rarely helps them process their feelings. Instead, ask them why they are so upset, and help them understand the source of their problem.

It's also important to pay attention to how your child responds to your methods. If they seem to withdraw and go quiet, or if they only get more upset, you may need to reevaluate your approach. Each child is an individual, and what works for one might not work for another. Rather than continuing to use a tactic that isn't working, be open to switching gears and looking for more creative solutions. For example, if they seem bored, try teaching through games and fun activities. If they are too angry to use their words, you can ask them to write their feelings down or draw a picture.

In all difficult interactions, you should remind your child that you're empathetic to their concerns and that you care about them. Sometimes we do things that upset our kids, like requiring they complete their chores before they can go outside and play. You should remain firm with these rules, but also ensure your child feels like their emotions are being validated and not dismissed. If they get angry about their chores, you could say, "I know they're not as fun as playtime, and I see that you're upset, but it really helps me when you clean up after yourself. Can you help out even though you want to play more? Maybe we can turn clean-up into a game too."

As kids get older, it's a good idea to give them some agency and let them flex their problem-solving muscles. Instead of deciding on a solution to the conflict yourself and telling them what to do, allow them to decide. For example, if your child is upset and having trouble calming down, you might ask them, "What kind of activity would you like to do to relax?" and let them choose if they want to color, read, cuddle with you, or spend some time alone in their room depending on what they feel they need. This way, you are both working through the experience, and you show your child you trust them to figure out their own emotional needs with your help.

Here are a few more basic tasks you can do at home to support the development of emotional intelligence:

- **Show empathy**: Work to understand why your child feels the way they do and demonstrate that you care about their opinions.
- **Be a model for appropriate expression of emotions**: Set a good example for your child. Be honest with your own emotions, and manage them appropriately without letting them overtake you.
- **Teach healthy coping skills**: Give your child plenty of options for how to express themselves and calm themselves down that don't cause harm to themselves or others.
- **Turn emotional intelligence into an ongoing goal**: There is no threshold at which you can stop learning more about emotional intelligence. Take active steps to teach it, and always be open to expanding your child's

knowledge and helping them practice their emotional intelligence skills.

- **Discuss challenges**: If your child is going through a difficult life situation or you notice they're having trouble with a certain emotion, set time aside to talk to them and come up with a solution together.
- **Work on your strategies for coping with emotions**: Evaluate the effectiveness of your coaching strategies and make adjustments when it seems like your child isn't getting the full benefit out of your lessons. Ask them if they think you could improve your approach in some way, and keep an eye out for times when you might slip back into dismissal or disapproval.
- **Help others**: Teach your child to be a positive force in their friend group and community by helping others, whether you volunteer for an organization or lend the neighbors a helping hand. Comfort others when they need support, and your child will learn to follow in your footsteps.

These are just a few of the many different ways you can encourage emotional growth. As you practice being an emotion coach for your child, you'll get a feeling for what works, what doesn't, and how you can adjust your methods to help your child succeed.

GAMES FOR ENCOURAGING EMOTIONAL INTELLIGENCE

In addition to the exercises mentioned above, you can also use games to teach your child about emotional intelligence. Kids learn a lot while they're playing; this is why games have become so prevalent in the classroom. When kids are having fun, they're more receptive to new information, and their minds and bodies are engaged. They'll internalize lessons without even knowing it, which means practicing emotional intelligence will come naturally to them in real-life situations.

Conversational EQ Game

The Conversational EQ Card Game is best suited for kids five or older. It is a special deck of cards decorated with different emotional discussion prompts and point values on the back. Players take turns drawing cards and performing the task on each one. Cards may have emotions and directions such as "I feel," I think," "ask permission," and "open question." The "I feel" and "I think" cards direct players to make an "I statement" about the emotion on the card. They might say, "I feel happy when mommy plays games with me," or, "I think meeting someone new can be scary." For the "ask permission" cards, the player should ask if it's okay for them to share their feelings, before saying an "I think" statement. For the "open question" cards, a player starts with an "I feel" sentence. Another player gets to ask them an open-ended question about that emotion, to which they must respond with an "I think" sentence.

The goal of the game is to get kids to practice putting their feelings into words. The "ask permission" cards teach them about when it is appropriate to have emotional conversations, and the "open discussion" cards get them into the habit of talking about their feelings with others.

Simon Says

Simon Says is a great game for building communication skills, as mentioned in *SHHHH...Listen!.* It is equally useful for emotional intelligence, as kids learn how to listen to others with an emotional twist. In Simon Says, one player is designated as "Simon," and they give commands to the other players. If they say "Simon says" before the instruction, the players should follow their directions. If they don't say "Simon says," they should do nothing. This is a great way to practice listening skills alongside emotional development.

To make Simon Says into a great emotional intelligence game, choose prompts that encourage kids to display different emotions. You might say, "Simon says make an angry face," "Simon says smile like you're really happy," or, "Simon says stand like you're confident." As kids get older, you can introduce more complicated emotions or ask kids to react like they would in different situations.

Self-Esteem Jenga

Helping your child build their self-esteem can assist them in having a healthier relationship with their emotions in turn. Kids who are self-confident are less guilty and fearful in regard to their emotions, and they have little trouble expressing themselves. They are emotionally honest, and they are often more likely to help others in need of assistance. Self-Esteem Jenga can teach kids confidence skills that form the backbone of their emotional intelligence.

Self-Esteem Jenga is similar to the usual game, where the tiles are built into a stack and players remove one tile at a time to keep the tower from toppling over. However, there is an added step of writing different prompts, tasks, and questions on the tiles before you build the tower. Each time someone removes a tile, they must complete the task written on it. Some ideas for prompts include talking about something that makes them happy, asking when the last time they got upset was, asking what skills they excel at, or having them come up with something their friends like about them. These boosts in self-confidence help kids see how their actions impact others and reduce feelings of shame and embarrassment.

Stop, Relax, and Think

Stop, Relax, and Think is a board game that helps kids make decisions about how they want to react when they feel various emotions. It can assist them in curbing impulsive behaviors, reminding them to calm down and think before they react. The game includes dice to roll as they move across a board, progressing through the four zones "feelings," "stop," "relax," and "think." They draw cards and collect points for completing various activities like answering questions about their emotions and listening to when others ask them to stop a certain behavior, which can help them practice the same behaviors when they face emotional turmoil in the real world.

The Fox and the Rabbit

The Fox and the Rabbit is a group game that is good for teaching self-management skills. The only supplies you need are two balls of different sizes or colors. One ball is designated as the "fox," while the other becomes the "rabbit." Have everyone stand in a circle and give each ball to kids on opposite sides of the circle. Kids can only hold either ball for a few seconds, and they shouldn't wait too long. The rabbit ball is trying to escape the fox, while the fox is trying to catch up to the rabbit. Kids must pass their ball in a way that helps it achieve its goal, based on where the other ball is.

This game is primarily about helping kids make decisions and take responsibility for their choices. Passing the ball the wrong way could result in the fox catching the rabbit, or widening the gap between the two. It also encourages kids to pay attention to what others are doing when they make their own choices, then react accordingly.

Which Emotion am I?

In this game, kids each get a card with the name of an emotion on it. They attach the card to their forehead with a rubber band or other headband without looking at it. The other kids must then help them guess which emotion is on their card by making the corresponding facial expression. If someone's card says "anger," the other kids might frown and puff out their cheeks. This teaches all players to model emotions and also to recognize others' emotional displays.

The Social and Emotional Competence Game

This is another board game tailor-made for teaching emotional intelligence. The board is divided into five sections, which are "communication," "caring," cooperating," "getting along," and "sharing feelings." Kids are encouraged to practice various skills related to each section, which helps them learn how to form and maintain healthy relationships with their peers and adults. Questions include conflict management, showing compassion, and team-building exercises.

Playing any of these games with your kids gives them a safe way to practice different emotional skills. You can also come up with fun games of your own that teach similar lessons, so long as they help you start a conversation about feelings with your child.

3

DO YOU NEED EMOTIONAL INTELLIGENCE IN THE CURRICULUM?

Parents play a large part in teaching kids about emotional intelligence, but this education doesn't just happen inside the home. It's also part of the education kids receive at school, whether inside the classroom or out on the playground. As kids start attending school, they might make their first friends outside their family, and their social circles will start to grow. They'll also probably experience their first arguments with people their own age, and learn how to apologize and compromise to help everyone get what they want.

Since kids learn so much about social interactions naturally at school, many teachers have started adopting lessons geared toward teaching emotional intelligence. This can reduce conflicts in the classroom and help kids manage their emotions so they can remain focused and motivated on their schoolwork. Many educators who view emotional intelligence as an important skill and know that it may even outrank the impact of IQ have started to use emotion-based lesson plans to provide kids with the skills they need to succeed throughout their lives. As our understanding of the importance of EQ deepens, emotional intelligence lessons become more and more prominent in the classroom.

Parents and guardians can also benefit from learning more about emotional intelligence curriculum in schools. This information can show you what to look for when selecting a school district for your child, and also enable you to talk with your child's teachers about their development and the types of teaching strategies they're using in the classroom. Even if you're not an educator, you should still learn about these new teaching styles, as you'll be better equipped to ensure your child is getting the best possible education.

WHY EMOTIONS MATTER IN EDUCATION

Teachers are important authority figures in kids' lives. Many of their earliest memories take place at school, and because teachers are responsible for their education, many kids come to see their kindergarten and early elementary school teachers as a source of guidance. Because of this, educators have a unique position from which they can help kids learn emotional intelligence. More and more schools are adopting techniques for increasing EQ in the younger grade levels, and for good reason. If the goal of education is to prepare kids with the skills they'll need to achieve success, then no lesson can be more important than emotional intelligence. On top of that, improvements in emotional intelligence can translate into cognitive intelligence, better grades, and greater motivation and focus.

How Emotions Can Impact Academic Success

Kids' emotional experiences have a significant impact on their academic careers. As previously mentioned, their level of mastery over their emotions can affect how motivated they are to work on classroom assignments and homework. If a child is struggling to deal with their emotions, they'll often find themselves too distracted to pay attention in class, and they may have trouble maintaining their focus on their assignments. A child who lacks emotional intelligence coaching may have a difficult time internalizing information as well because they aren't fully engaged in the lesson. Issues with attention and focus can make it much harder for a child to do well in school, so they should be addressed in all classrooms.

Part of this process involves cultivating a positive environment for learning. It's difficult for kids to learn when they feel stressed and uncomfortable, and it can be just as hard if they're going through a rough time in their lives and they try to suppress these emotions. Teachers can implement an exercise for emotional honesty such as using a classroom mood meter, which allows kids to point to different moods to describe how they're feeling in regard to their level of energy and how positive or negative they feel. This helps them see when mismanaged negative emotions might be holding a child back. Instead of proceeding with class as usual, "Taking time to recognize feelings, elaborate on their causes, and jointly brainstorm potential strategies to shift or maintain them helps ensure that adults and children use emotions effectively to create a climate supportive of learning" (Tominey, O'Bryon, Rivers, & Shapses, 2017, para. 7). When every child in a classroom is at a comfortable energy level and there are no significant emotions pulling them away from their studies, they are ready to learn.

Different emotional states can have an impact on a child's performance in school. Kids who are enjoying their studies and are hopeful about their ability to improve their grades are more likely to work hard, as are kids who are encouraged to take pride in their work. Kids may be held back by persistent feelings of anger, worry, self-doubt, and boredom, disengaging from the lesson. It's important that the classroom atmosphere encourages kids to enjoy their time spent at school. Any emotions that prevent them from doing so should be discussed and resolved so kids get the most out of each day.

Academic anxieties can also distract and discourage kids from doing their best. Some kids may struggle with a certain subject, such as reading or math. If they don't get the adequate extra support they need to catch up with the rest of the class, they can start to feel discouraged, which only makes it harder for them to pay attention and follow along with each lesson. This can, in turn, impact their performance on tests, the way they approach questions on exams and homework, and the subject they choose to major in or pursue for their career. However, these anxieties can be eased through emotional intelligence training. Some studies of child neuroscience show that "math deficits resulting from anxiety are eliminated in individuals who show activation of brain areas related to cognitive control and motivation" (Trezise, 2017, para. 2). In other words, the better a child is at handling their emotions, the easier they'll find it to let these academic anxieties go so they can focus on self-improvement.

How Classroom Factors Impact Emotions

Various factors may affect how well kids are able to adapt to school and how much they gain from each lesson. Classroom factors, external factors, and individual factors all have an impact on academic success for kids.

Classroom factors are the easiest for educators to control and adjust to suit kids' needs. These include the type of environment in the classroom and the contents of the curriculum. Classroom environments that are warm, inviting, and free of tension generally have a positive impact on kids' abilities to learn. It's a good idea for teachers to encourage questions, even if they may seem silly or simple, as this allows kids to ask for clarification without any fear of being teased. Teachers should also make emotional expression a part of the class through various discussions and projects, as this provides a healthy outlet for kids who may have a difficult time at home.

External factors may help or impede a child's ability to succeed academically as well. They include things like home life and different social interactions. A bad argument at recess can bother a child while they're trying to focus on their studies, as can an argument they had with their parent or guardian. A tough event like the death of a loved one or the divorce of their parents could also make it hard to concentrate if kids don't know how to properly deal with these feelings. While teachers can't control the home lives of the kids in their classes, they can provide a helping hand where it is appropriate, listening to kids' concerns and pointing them toward healthy outlets for their emotions.

Finally, there are individual factors to consider for each child. No two kids are exactly alike, and they may have different educational needs. Some kids may benefit from hands-on learning, while others may prefer a more traditional classroom approach. Some will be shy and withdrawn, while others will be so outgoing they may try to chatter with friends through their classes. In addition to general disposition, there may be genetic factors impacting their social skills or cognitive abilities that vary from child to child. Adjusting for these factors can be tough, as there's no "one size fits all" approach. Spending time connecting with each child as an individual, imparting emotional intelligence skills to help them communicate their preferences and what they're comfortable with, can help teachers find the right way to support each child in their class.

There are multiple possible models educators can use to bring emotional intelligence lessons into the classroom. Each represents a different approach to instructing various social and emotional skills, with some focusing more heavily on the lesson plans themselves and others aiming to create a classroom environment conducive to learning these principles. Some notable models include Maslow's hierarchy of needs, social-emotional learning, and the Ruler approach.

MASLOW'S HIERARCHY OF NEEDS AND EDUCATION

Maslow's hierarchy of needs is a theory from the mid-1900s that arranges humans' most basic needs as a five-tier list, with the needs of the highest significance on the bottom. Each tier must be fulfilled before the next one can be achieved. Starting from the base of the tiered pyramid that is used to depict the model, the needs are "physiological, safety, love and belonging, esteem, and self-actualization" (McLeod, 2020, para. 2). Physiological needs are needs that must be fulfilled for our physical well-being. They include water, food, sleep, and warmth, without which we would die. After that are the safety and security needs, and then the need for social connections. Esteem involves feelings of accomplishment and pride in one's work, while at the top of the pyramid, self-actualization refers to finding a sense of purpose and engaging in creative activities.

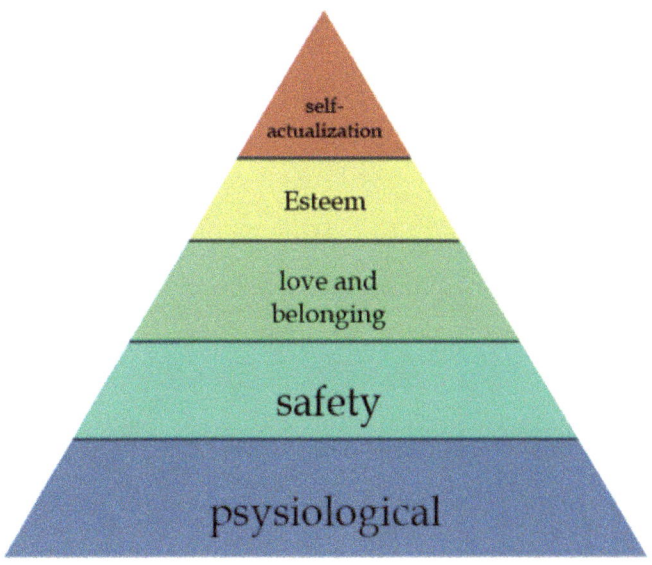

According to Maslow's theory, everyone's needs follow this hierarchy, even and especially kids. Recently, it has been applied to the classroom, to show how fulfilling some or all of these needs can help kids focus on their studies. For example, a child who is hungry, perhaps because their family might not be able to afford to send them in with a filling and nutritious meal for lunch, is likely to be distracted by their hunger and have a harder time learning. The same is true for kids who lack a close social group and may not feel their "love and belonging" needs are being met. Until all needs are fulfilled, they will find it harder to learn.

Once kids' basic needs are met, they can then start feeling motivation and curiosity about new subjects. This is yet another example of the impact emotions have on kids' abilities to pay attention and learn at school. Physical safety, emotional safety, and social acceptance are all mandatory parts of a supportive classroom environment. Kids who are shown they are respected and valued, and who have high self-esteem, will be able to progress faster emotionally and cognitively than kids who find their classroom environments to be alienating or even antagonistic to their ability to learn.

Benefits of Emotional Intelligence on Classroom Performance

Kids who are better versed in emotional intelligence experience a wide range of benefits in the classroom. As previously mentioned, they usually have an easier time paying attention because their emotional needs are met and they aren't bothered by unresolved, uncontrollable emotions. In addition to this, many emotionally intelligent kids are more engaged in their school lessons and more excited to learn. They tend to have more positive relationships with their peers and teachers, and they're often more compassionate and empathetic, which strengthens these social bonds.

Kids who excel at emotional intelligence also tend to excel at managing themselves, as well as relating to those around them. They usually have fewer difficulties staying motivated, even without external motivating factors like the threat of bad grades or deadlines. Their communication skills are typically better as well, as they better understand how their fellow students feel. This can help them come into themselves as capable, confident learners who aren't too embarrassed to ask for help when they need it.

All of these factors combine to yield kids who are in control of their emotions, great at maintaining social relationships, and who have few academic troubles. Kids who lack emotional intelligence skills may struggle with many of these tasks. They may feel disconnected from school, which can hurt their grades and leave them feeling isolated from their peers. The best way to ensure every child has a chance to succeed in the classroom and that they aren't a distraction for their fellow students is to support their emotional growth.

SOCIAL-EMOTIONAL LEARNING

Social-emotional learning (SEL) has been shown to have significant long-term positive effects on kids. It is "the process of developing the self-awareness, self-control, and interpersonal skills that are vital for school, work, and life success" (Committee for Children, n.d., para. 1). Developing these skills helps people of all ages manage everyday difficulties and challenges. With SEL, kids discover self-discipline, problem-solving, emotional management, and impulse control skills that directly impact their success academically, socially, and later, professionally.

Some schools have started to adopt a systematic approach to SEL in all subjects. This involves striving to create a caring and fair learning environment that encourages participation from everyone, as well as collaboration between students. Exercises for building social and emotional skills are infused into nearly every aspect of kids' daily lives, so they are always learning and practicing whether they are in class or at home in their communities. More than two decades of research has shown the many benefits of SEL, which include a 20% decrease in bullying, a 42% decrease in physical aggression, a 5-12% decrease in dropout rates in schools that adopted this policy, and a 13% increase in academic achievements among the student bodies of these schools (Committee for Children, n.d., para. 8). This method routinely increases academic achievement, preparedness for continuing education, and career success, while decreasing behavioral issues, teen drug use and pregnancy, and mental health problems. By making emotional intelligence a more prominent and consistent part of the curriculum, kids have fewer behavioral issues and are better able to pursue personal and academic success.

The CASEL Wheel and Competencies

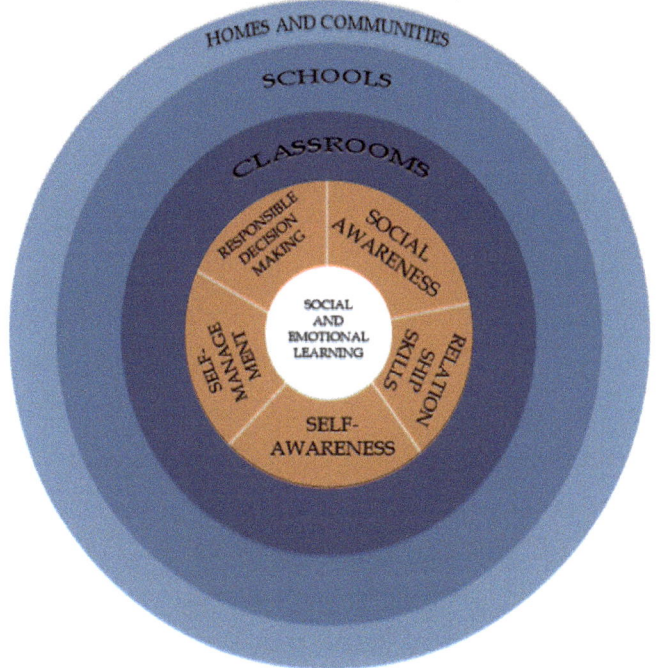

The Collaborative for Academic, Social, and Emotional Learning (CASEL) has been at the forefront of SEL for more than 20 years. In this time, they have developed a framework for SEL known as the CASEL wheel. It is based on a number of different competencies kids learn from their communities, families, schools, and classrooms. Each of these locations for learning forms an outer ring of the wheel. Starting with communities and moving inwards, the corresponding skills kids can learn are aligned learning opportunities through community programs, authentic partnerships with family members, a sense of schoolwide culture and policies, and SEL instruction in the classroom. Other key skills that make up the middle section of the wheel are self-awareness, self-management, responsible decision-making, relationship skills, and social awareness, with social and emotional learning at the core of the wheel (CASEL, n.d., para. 4).

The CASEL wheel is useful for visualizing how each aspect of a child's life affects their development. The skills toward the center of the circle are those that are most heavily enforced by educators, while the skills in the outer rings come from external sources. The wheel helps teachers identify the skills they should prioritize while still accounting for learning opportunities outside the classroom.

Approaches to SEL

SEL can vary a bit from school to school, as each educator prioritizes different learning goals. Ideally, effective approaches to SEL should include four different elements. They should be sequenced, active, focused, and explicit (CASEL, n.d., para. 3). This ideal approach is often shortened to the acronym "SAFE." Let's break each part down to better understand the important role it plays.

A sequenced approach means that the activities taught throughout each school year and between the different grade levels are coordinated in an order that makes sense. Younger kids start with easier to grasp foundation concepts and the complexity increases with time and practice. Kids don't repeat lessons for longer than it takes for them to internalize them, so they don't become bored and disengaged. They also aren't pushed to learn difficult concepts too soon, and each new idea builds off the previous one to guide kids through the lessons.

SEL should involve active lessons and nontraditional forms of learning to maintain kids' attention. Just like the games for learning emotional intelligence we discussed in the previous chapter, with more creative approaches, kids are more inclined to practice their SEL skills without feeling like they're doing work. This means they'll keep at it until they've really mastered them.

SEL teaching methods often benefit from being focused as well. It's difficult to teach many kids about emotional intelligence all at once, especially since each child may have different strengths and weaknesses. Creating a lesson plan more tailored to each child makes sure everyone is able to benefit from SEL, not just those who excel in a typical school environment.

The last important component of SEL is keeping the lessons explicit. All activities should target a specific emotional or social skill, and teachers should help kids understand how the lessons they complete translate into real-world skills with a brief recap at the end. It can help to ask kids what they feel they learned, as this makes it easier to identify if the lessons have been explicit enough.

These four components form the backbone of SEL in schools across the nation. As long as they are present, teachers may experiment with unique variations and different approaches. Some common approaches include the use of stand-alone lessons targeting a specific aspect of emotional and social competence, repeated practices such as project-based learning and cooperative assignments that build teamwork skills, and the full integration of SEL into all subjects in the curriculum. Especially dedicated schools might take this idea even further and perform a full organizational overhaul, turning SEL into a school-wide initiative to make the school's climate and culture as a whole more conducive to cognitive and emotional learning.

How SEL Skills Are Being Trained in the Classroom

SEL is a fairly recent development in most schools, so there is still plenty of ongoing training as schools begin to shift over to a more emotional intelligence-heavy curriculum. Most teachers in these schools must undergo special training before their lesson plans start to fully accommodate social and emotional skills. In schools with SEL-based curriculums, teachers are also instructed to find opportunities to reinforce these lessons throughout the day through repeated practice. For example, if students learn about sharing in the morning, they might later receive an assignment that requires them to trade supplies with other students. Kids learn a lesson, then get a chance to showcase what they've learned in a real-world scenario.

Teachers can also foster these kinds of skills in their students through their natural interactions during the school day. If a child comes up complaining that one of their playmates hurt their feelings, this can become a chance to help both kids practice their conflict resolution skills. By using a student-centered approach to instruction, teachers can have one-on-one conversations with their students and assess their emotional intelligence skills.

Some after-school programs that focus on SEL have also shown to be beneficial to kids' emotional and social skills. After-school programs naturally give kids an outlet for hyperactive emotions and a place to socialize, but they can also be of great help in reinforcing emotional intelligence lessons. These programs often reduce the frequency of problem behaviors like disrupting a lesson or getting into fights with other kids. They have the potential to greatly improve kids' self-esteem and how they view themselves, connectedness between all the school's students, grades and test scores, and positive social behaviors.

THE RULER APPROACH

Recognizing, Understanding, Labeling, Expressing, and Regulating emotions, also known as the RULER approach, was developed by Marc Brackett in 2005 in the Yale Center for Emotional Intelligence. It is an evidence-based method for teaching emotional intelligence that focuses on making the classroom climate as hospitable as possible. It involves integrating emotional recognition and identification into all aspects of the classroom. The approach not only improves student emotional intelligence but also often improves relationships between teachers and administrators, as well as the school at large.

Five Skills of Emotional Intelligence

The RULER approach's acronym is short for five different skills relating to emotional intelligence. Each skill is necessary for kids to learn in order to foster a positive classroom environment.

Recognizing Emotions in Oneself and Others

The recognizing part of the approach encourages kids to consider how they are feeling at any given time. Kids should ask themselves, "How do I feel right now? How can my feelings affect others?" They should also learn to identify physical signs of different emotions, such as their energy level, breathing rate, posture, and heart rate.

Understanding the Causes and Consequences of Emotions

To understand their emotions, kids should ask themselves, "Why do I feel this way? What will happen if I continue to feel this way and don't do anything about it?" They should learn how to identify different events, people, and thoughts that can affect their emotions so they can better anticipate and react to them.

Labeling Emotions With a Nuanced Vocabulary

In the labeling portion of the RULER approach, kids learn to give their feelings names. Older kids should use a more descriptive, specific vocabulary. For example, while "sad" might be a good enough descriptor for very young kids, eventually it will be more useful to use terms like "lonely," "hurt," "dejected," or "regretful" for clearer communication. This also helps kids identify the root cause of their feelings so they can come up with a specific management strategy.

Expressing Emotions in Line With Cultural Norms and Social Context

Expression of emotions must be tailored to the situation kids are currently in. If they're alone in their room, it's okay to yell into a pillow. If they're out in public, disruptive yelling or other, more aggressive reactions aren't appropriate. Kids should learn that different forms of emotional expression can help in different contexts, and they should develop a variety of different coping mechanisms they can use in each situation.

Regulating Emotions With Helpful Strategies

In the regulating portion of the RULER method, kids ask themselves, "What should I do to either maintain or ease my current feelings? What kinds of behaviors should I engage in, and which should I avoid?" Teachers can provide kids with both short-term and long-term strategies.

Some strategies kids can use to regulate their emotions include:

- Repeating an encouraging phrase or mantra to stay determined and motivated
- Practicing a breathing exercise to calm down
- Giving others the benefit of the doubt when they do or say things they don't mean

- Physically separating themselves from the source of stress
- Talking to friends, parents, or teachers for support and stress relief

Anchors of Emotional Intelligence

There are four tools that are frequently used to help convey emotional intelligence skills to kids in the RULER method. These are the Charter, the Meta Moment, the Mood Meter, and the Blueprint.

The Charter is a community-created document where everyone writes down ideas and pledges about how they intend to treat each other. It functions as a social contract that provides guidelines for acceptable behaviors in the classroom. Each child gets a say in deciding the respectful rules of the classroom that work best for everyone.

The Meta Moment is used when there are strong emotions. Kids take a step back from the situation and consider their options before impulsively reacting. They learn to choose actions that showcase their "best self," replacing harmful or ineffective reactions with more empowering ones.

The Mood Meter helps kids use more descriptive words to explain their feelings. Instead of simply saying they're "fine," kids learn to use language like "calm," "peaceful," or "excited."

The Mood Meter has two axes, with one representing their energy levels and the other showing how pleasant or unpleasant their current feelings are. Once kids decide where they fall on the Mood Meter, they can then describe their feelings in more detail.

Mood Meter

Nervous Worried 　　　Angry	Excited Cheerful
Lonely 　　Sad 　 Hopeless	Content Calm 　　　Serene

Energy Level (y-axis)
Positivity (x-axis)

The Blueprint encourages two people involved in an argument to see things from the other person's point of view. They consider how someone else might be feeling, while still acknowledging their own emotions as valid. This assists in finding a solution that works for everyone.

There are many different methods for integrating emotional intelligence into education. Whether schools stick to basic emotional education, incorporate SEL approaches, or make use of the RULER method, it's clear that emotional education has a place in the classroom and greatly benefits students.

4

COPING WITH AGGRESSIVE OR DEFIANT KIDS THE SMART WAY

It can be much harder to deal with an aggressive child than it is to manage a sad or reserved one. Oftentimes, aggressive kids may hurt you, other members of the family, their friends, or themselves. These behaviors are unacceptable in any situation. While it is fine for kids to be angry, they should never lash out and try to hurt someone, nor should they destroy property or antagonize their peers.

Aggressive behaviors aren't just harmful for others. They can also put kids at a significant social disadvantage, as they gain a reputation for being mean. Other kids might avoid them, and they may have trouble making and maintaining friendships as a result. They may have trouble learning social skills because they can't easily practice them with close friends. If you're the parent of an aggressive child, you may even find yourself feeling emotionally distanced from them despite your best efforts to love and support them.

Managing aggressive behavior usually requires formal, serious intervention. You may need to curb harmful behaviors including defiance, violence, disruptive behaviors, oppositional behaviors, temper tantrums, and meltdowns. These may occur publicly or inside the home. Either way, young kids who exhibit these aggressive tendencies need to learn alternate methods to communicate their frustrations. You can help guide them as they learn to regulate their impulses and emotional expressions by showing them what kind of behavior is expected from them and what actions are not acceptable.

REASONS FOR ACTING OUT

Dealing with an aggressive child can be exhausting at times. It is all too easy to see their behaviors as purposefully malicious and to lose your temper with them, just as they have lost their temper with you. You may even be tempted to blame the bad behavior on your child simply being a bad kid who is predisposed to violence and aggression. However, this method of thinking assumes that there is nothing you can do to limit the aggression, taking away both your agency and your child's agency. This can be very harmful, as you may start to allow these behaviors to go unchecked because you feel powerless. Alternatively, you might resort to strict punishments without trying to understand why the bad behavior is occurring. Either response only encourages kids to act out further.

The key to understanding why your child is acting out is to see it not as a purposeful, spiteful action, but instead as a bad reaction to some unmet need or other difficulty in your child's life. Aggressive behaviors may stem from all kinds of sources in kids. Just as you might be more standoffish and have a higher tendency to snap if you're feeling exhausted, stressed, or unfulfilled, so too do kids. Most aggressive kids lack the vocabulary or emotional understanding necessary to communicate their problem to you in a healthy way, so they resort to aggression. Therefore, the best way to root out aggressive behaviors is to start by figuring out why they are occurring.

Some possible sources of childhood aggression include:

- Unmet physical needs, such as hunger or exhaustion
- An upsetting situation like bullying at school, parental divorce, or the passing of a loved one
- Mental health conditions such as post-traumatic stress disorder or depression
- Learning disabilities
- Fear or anxiety about something in their lives
- A desire to impress their peers
- Overcompensating for a lack of confidence
- Seeking attention, especially if your child feels like they are often overlooked
- A lack of agency over their lives
- A failure to understand limits of acceptable behavior
- Overstimulation
- Mirroring your behaviors or the behaviors of other adults in their lives

How to Identify the Root Cause of Anger

Many experts suggest that looking for the root cause of anger in kids provides the greatest benefits when trying to ease aggression. If you're uncertain why your child might be acting this way, look for any common factors in their aggressive outbursts. Do they tend to occur right after they come home from school, before they leave in the mornings, or only at school? Do they act more aggressively when they've spent time around certain people? Is there a specific situation that often leads your child to become aggressive? Does the behavior repeat itself around the same time of day?

Try to identify any patterns in the behavior, as this might provide more information about why they're getting aggressive. For example, if a child's aggression comes from schoolyard bullies, they might get in fights at school or be in an especially horrible mood shortly after they get home. Once you've figured out why the aggression is occurring, you can then decide whether a conversation or a punishment is necessary. You just may find that talking to your child about the difficulties they're facing may get you further than putting them in time-out or taking away a privilege each time they act out.

Bullying is a serious issue that can significantly impact your child's emotional intelligence and ability to succeed in a number of ways. If you believe your child's aggression may stem from bullying, it's important to be proactive in getting the bullying to stop. We will discuss how to identify signs your child is being bullied and steps you can take as a parent to resolve the issue in Chapter 6.

TIPS FOR MAINTAINING A CONFIDENT, CONSTRUCTIVE OUTLOOK AS A PARENT

Even when you understand where your child's anger is coming from, it can be hard to keep a level head when you see them acting aggressively. It's natural for us to see aggressive behavior and mirror it ourselves, but this doesn't help our kids. If they yell and we start yelling right back, we've devolved the situation into a screaming match that's sure to end in tears for one or both parties. It's important to try to stay as rational and responsible as possible when your child has a tantrum or lashes out in another way. This makes it much easier to identify the cause of the anger and take steps to correct the behavior without going overboard.

If you read *SHHHH...Listen!,* you'll be familiar with this idea. If you want to help your child calm down and let go of aggressive feelings, you must first let these aggressive feelings go yourself. Only then can you effectively coach them through their emotions. Here are a few different methods and tips you can use to regain your cool when your child frustrates you.

Don't Take it Personally

If you go through life always assuming the worst from others, you may find yourself provoking negative reactions. This is also true when it comes to kids. If you anticipate your child will behave badly, or if you make judgmental and hostile decisions regarding your child's ability to control their anger, you might just end up creating the very reaction you were hoping to avoid. Nobody likes to feel like someone's just waiting for them to slip up, least of all young kids who struggle to control their angrier impulses. Avoid making negative judgments about your child before they act out or assuming their behavior is meant to purposefully aggravate you. If you're not careful, you can create a self-fulfilling prophecy.

If you find yourself feeling hurt and defensive because of your child's behaviors, take a step back and remind yourself that there's more at play here than it may seem on the surface. Avoid taking these bad behaviors as personal attacks. This helps you keep calm when tantrums occur and avoid provoking aggression in otherwise benign situations. It can also support a healthier relationship between you and your child free of mistrust and hurt feelings. Additionally, you'll avoid harming your child's long-term development by teaching them to internalize the idea that they're predisposed to being bad. By not taking things personally, you give your child the opportunity to change their behavior.

Be Realistic About Your Child's Ability to Remember Rules

We often expect kids to have the same cognitive abilities as adults, but this just isn't fair. Kids' memories are not nearly as well-developed when they are young, especially if they are struggling with emotional issues. They often get distracted, and they may break rules not out of a sense of spite, but simply because they forgot. While you should still uphold your rules, reminding yourself that genuine forgetfulness could be at play allows you to avoid enacting a punishment for a simple mistake.

Keep an eye on the pace at which your child's emotional intelligence improves, as well as which abilities they've mastered and which they've yet to get a solid grasp on. When necessary, provide calm, patient reminders, and try to remind kids of rules when they become relevant. For example, you might remind your child to share right before they start playing with a friend or sibling. This way, all the rules are laid out for your child, and they only need to follow them to meet your expectations.

Be Realistic About Your Child's Developments in Empathy and Kindness

Just as kids may take a while to fully internalize new rules or figure out how they should act in a given situation, so too do they need time to develop and utilize empathy, especially if you've just started trying to correct their aggressive behaviors. If you notice your child fails to show concern for others in some circumstances, it's likely the result of some misunderstanding rather than malice. Many kids might perceive the situation differently than how you see it, or they lack control over their impulses and act without thinking. This can lead to them causing harm without recognizing it or stopping themselves in time. Your child might also lash out because they're experiencing another source of emotional pain, just as you might snap at someone when you're having a bad day and feel overworked.

It's important to remind your child about the limits of acceptable behaviors, but keep in mind that there will be good and bad days. Your child may show great strides in empathy one day and struggle with it the next. This doesn't mean all of your efforts were for nothing; they just haven't yet had enough opportunities to practice kindness and empathy. The more experience they have dealing with conflict and practicing kindness, the better they will become at consistently being considerate of others. Some common opportunities to learn that may benefit your child include developing a safe and secure relationship with you and the rest of the family, discussing feelings and how other people hint at their emotions, being around positive emotional role models, and growing up in an environment that reinforces and provides rewards for cooperation and self-control.

Focus on Maintaining a Positive Relationship

It's sometimes more beneficial to pick and choose your battles than it is to lay out consistent punishments. Consider each situation by its own merits. Was your child being intentionally cruel or aggressive, or were there other factors at play? Would punishing your child in this instance hurt them more than it would help them? These are important questions to ask, as you never want to damage your relationship with your child if you can help it. Sometimes this means foregoing a punishment, though you should still point out when their behaviors aren't acceptable.

Many studies support the idea that positive reinforcement is better at delivering the desired outcome than punishing bad behaviors. Kids typically want to please their parents, and they'll take actions they think will make you happy. If you reward them for good behaviors, they're more likely to repeat those actions. On the other hand, strict punishments could distance you from your child as they learn to fear your reaction. They may start to act dishonestly to avoid punishment rather than actually exhibiting good behaviors for praise, which can seriously harm your attempts to guide their development.

You may find more success with the Oregon Model, which involves "weekly sessions of coaching and role-playing" that teach parents "effective ways to set limits, foster cooperation, settle arguments in a constructive way, and inject daily life with pleasant, loving activities" (Dewar, 2016, para. 47). This can help you avoid framing your parent-child relationship around negativity and the avoidance of consequences, and instead encourage you to use positive reinforcement more often.

Don't Sacrifice Your Own Psychological Well-Being

As parents, we tend to put our kids' needs ahead of our own. This can be especially frustrating when it feels like we're running ourselves ragged and all of our efforts are changing very little about our kids' behaviors. We may begin to view their actions as ungrateful, and in some cases start to resent them. This can all lead to a great deal of guilt and stress. While wanting your child to have a good life and leave their aggressive tendencies behind is a noble pursuit, it shouldn't come at the cost of your own health. The more stressed you are, the less patience you'll have for your child's outbursts, and the harder it will be to deal with them fairly.

Take breaks when you need them. Treat your well-being as just as significant of a priority as your child's well-being, and don't push yourself to the brink of exhaustion when dealing with your child. This will only put additional strain on your relationship. Care for yourself and enlist the help of others when you need to take a moment to recover. By looking after your mental and physical health, you'll be in a better position to assist your child in doing the same.

12 EVIDENCE-BASED TIPS FOR HANDLING AGGRESSION, DEFIANCE, AND ACTING OUT

Now that you know the importance of your mindset and some of the things you should avoid doing, you can turn your attention to things you should be doing to help your child let go of their anger. Keep in mind that while all of these tips are helpful, none of them are miraculous solutions that will yield instantaneous results. You'll need to be consistent, and you may need to repeat exercises for multiple months before you start seeing noticeable changes. However, if you stick with these strategies and you keep a level head, you're sure to see your child's behavior gradually improve over time.

Keep Kids From Overtaxing Themselves

If your child is having difficulty learning social-emotional skills, it might not be a good idea to expose them to potential sources of conflict too frequently. Your child might be able to behave themselves during the first or second interactions, but if something continues to frustrate or upset them, they may lose their temper and end up acting aggressively just because they've overtaxed themselves. It's a good idea to guide your child away from the source of their stress when you see they might be about to lash out and give them a moment to collect themselves.

For example, let's say you've noticed your child is great for the first 20 minutes of a playdate with their friend, but they start to get grouchy around the 30 minute mark. Rather than letting things progress until they lose control of their emotions, consider stepping in and cutting the playdate short. This leaves both kids seeing the interaction as a positive experience without any tears. Over time, your child's tolerance and self-control will increase, allowing them to enjoy longer playdates.

Remember the Big Picture

One of the most important things to remember is that social relationships form the bedrock of healthy interactions for your child. Kids who don't get adequately socialized are more likely to have behavioral problems because they aren't used to interacting with others. All positive relationships your child forms help them improve their emotional skills and stay connected to their friends and family members.

As a parent or guardian, you are one of the most important relationships for any child. If you're a parent, you are the first person your child ever bonded with. This is incredibly significant, as your relationship provides the blueprint for how all future relationships will go. Encourage your child to continue expanding their social circle as they grow up and meet new people, but ensure the parent-child bond remains strong at all times.

Understand Why Kids Push Back

When your child is disobedient, what is your gut reaction? There's a good chance that you assume they're being defiant on purpose. While they may know they're doing something they're not supposed to, kids rarely choose to act disobediently for no reason at all. They may be upset about something you said or did, or there may be another reason why they're reluctant to do as you ask. Pause, collect yourself, and see if you can get them to tell you why they're refusing your request rather than jumping to anger and punishment.

It's common for many kids to resist going to school when they're young. They may resist your efforts to get them ready and in the car or on the bus in the morning. Instead of getting frustrated with them, ask them why they don't want to go to school. You might find that they're experiencing a problem at school with bullies or with difficulty learning the material, or possibly just that they're anxious about being separated from you and they haven't yet made friends with their classmates. With this new information, you can alter your approach to help them feel more comfortable leaving for school, which often results in them enjoying their time at school more as well.

Reinforce Self-Control With Games

Just as you can use games to teach kids general emotional intelligence, you can also use them for reducing aggression. Using the medium of games encourages kids to listen and follow directions. It keeps a learning experience fun and makes the values instilled by these games easier to remember. Additionally, playing games with your child is a great way to spend time with them while encouraging their cognitive and emotional development.

There are many games you can play that help you impart lessons about aggression. You might choose a game that lets them work out excessive energy through harmless exercise. You can also encourage them to talk about what upsets them with the Conversational EQ Game, or roleplay different situations like dealing with bullies and having a disagreement with their friends.

Look After Yourself

Too much stress interferes with your ability to be a good teacher and parent. It's often said that you don't get a sick day when your job is being a parent, but this mentality isn't healthy. Needing a break doesn't make you a bad parent, nor does it mean you've given up on helping your child. Get some rest by doing calming activities you enjoy like reading, watching some TV, or taking a spa day while you let another family member watch your child for a brief time. Once you feel relaxed and centered, you'll be better at handling your child's aggression without getting fed up yourself.

Get Some Rest

Too little sleep makes all of us cranky and more prone to frustration. If you're tired, you're more likely to say something unkind you'll regret later. This is also true for kids, who need even more sleep than adults do. Toddlers may need as much as 12-14 hours of sleep per day to be at their best, while older kids still need around 10 hours and adults should get at least eight hours. Poor rest makes it harder to use your problem-solving skills and more likely that you and your child will resort to impulsive behaviors, which can further fracture self-control.

Foster Positive Sibling Relationships

If you have more than one child, you know how difficult it can be to dissuade sibling bickering. Sometimes your kids might get along like perfect angels, while other times they may be at each other's throats. It's important to remind all of your kids to be kind and compassionate to their siblings, even when they get frustrated with each other. Remind your kids that they're family and they need to look out for each other.

One great way to improve sibling relationships is to spend more time together as a family unit. You might have a family game night, take a weekend trip, or just make an effort to eat dinner together at the table each night. As your kids spend more time together and engage in shared interests, they'll be less likely to act aggressively toward each other and more likely to care for each other.

Defuse Negative Emotions With Reminders of Support

Kids may act out because they feel like they're alone and no one understands them. This is especially common when they start going to school, where they may feel like other kids don't like them if they're having trouble making friends. This can leave them feeling isolated and uncertain of their place in their peer group and their community.

The best way to ease this harm is to remind your child that they have people in their lives who love them and want them to succeed. Encourage them to reflect on your support and the support of the rest of the family when they need a reason to calm themselves down. As they continue practicing this method of self-soothing, they'll get into fewer conflicts and ease their aggressive tendencies, which will, in turn, help them connect with other kids and form an even larger support circle.

Help Kids Revise Their Negative Assumptions

Sometimes aggression stems from negative assumptions about how an interaction is going to go. You're probably familiar with this feeling yourself. Maybe you made plans to do something a little out of your comfort zone, and the closer it gets, the more you start regretting your decision. However, when you actually follow through on your plan, you see that you worked yourself up for no reason at all and things weren't so bad; maybe you even had fun. Kids are susceptible to making the same kinds of assumptions. They might resist spending time with other kids because they're worried about getting made fun of or being rejected, and this can make them lash out in aggression. But if you take a moment to help them see the situation as an opportunity to make new friends and encourage them to go into it with an open mind, they might find themselves pleasantly surprised.

Beware Mechanisms of Moral Disengagement

Some kids act aggressively because they don't yet have the empathy skills needed to understand how their actions hurt others, but this isn't true for all kids. Some may use aggression and fail to see how it's a bad thing because they've become convinced that what they're doing isn't bad at all. They might feel like the other person deserves their cruelty for some reason, or that it's necessary for them to achieve a certain goal. Remind your child that they're still causing harm and that everyone is deserving of basic decency from them no matter who they are.

As an example, consider a situation where your child's friend group is encouraging them to participate in the bullying of another student. Your child might know this is wrong on some level, but they also know that they need to do it to save face with their friends. However, if their friends are being bullies they're probably not good friends after all, and their actions are going to cause much more harm than good. Discuss the situation with your child and help them see that no one deserves to be bullied and they should take a stand against it, even if it creates a problem in their friend group.

Use Problem-Solving Disciplinary Tactics

Discipline is a method for correcting your child's behavior, but it can also cause unnecessary harm if you are too heavy-handed with your punishments. If your child frustrates you, you might be tempted to ground them, berate them, or even hit them. Beware punishments that do more to make you feel better than they do to help your child. Physical violence should never be part of your disciplinary method, and even groundings can be unnecessary if they don't get to the root of the problem. Instead, choose disciplinary measures that work to correct the bad behavior.

Let's say your child gets angry and shoves their plate off the table at dinner time, making a mess on the floor. You could choose to yell at them, which would leave you both frustrated and teach them very little. On the other hand, you could have them clean up the mess they made, teaching them the direct consequences of their actions and to take responsibility for the harm they cause. You could respond to a disagreement with a sibling by having them play nice with their brother or sister once they've calmed down. If your child hurts someone's feelings, just having them apologize can be enough for them to recognize how their words can help or hurt the people they care about. The punishment you dole out should be proportionate to the severity of the crime, and it should help kids recognize why their actions were wrong while giving them the opportunity to correct them.

Seek Professional Advice if Necessary

As much as we want to be the ones to help our kids, sometimes we are simply unequipped for the task. If your child has a learning disability or other special need, previously experienced trauma or is going through a traumatic experience, or if you believe there may be other unknown variables at work, there's nothing shameful about asking for the help of a professional. Child psychologists, pediatricians, and behavioral therapists can all help your child learn to express their emotions in a more positive way or provide alternate treatment methods that reduce aggression without harming your child.

DISCIPLINING YOUR CHILD

All discipline should be carried out with the goal of encouraging good behavior and replacing bad behaviors. Discipline should never occur because it makes you feel better or functions as a way for you to vent your own frustrations on your child. This kind of maladaptive discipline usually manifests in cruel words or physical violence, which helps neither of you and does little to swap bad behaviors for good ones in the future. Instead, it can contribute to a culture of mistrust and resentment in the family, which actively stands in the way of emotional intelligence development.

Every action has consequences, whether they're good or bad. Behavioral modifications should be built off the ideal principle that good behavior results in positive consequences, and bad behavior results in negative consequences. Kids should learn and understand this rule so they can anticipate how you'll react to whatever they do. You can modify the environment around your child to facilitate good behaviors and discourage bad ones with your punishments. For example, you might send a child to their room so they can take a moment to relax and calm down in a private, safe location after getting worked up. You might need to take away TV or video game privileges if you feel like these things are contributing to bad behaviors. Making environmental adjustments can have a much more significant impact on behavior than most harsher punishments, and it rarely breeds the same kind of distrust that can strain and fracture the parent-child relationship.

Different discipline methods can be broken down into three main categories: positive punishment, negative punishment, and positive reinforcement.

Positive Punishment

Positive punishment refers to any added consequence meant to deter kids from repeating bad behavior again in the future. The added consequence should reflect the type of infraction that occurred. You might find that adding an additional responsibility to your child's list of chores is an effective way to punish positively without harming your child. For example, if you find out your child was lying about putting their toys away, a positive punishment method might be telling them they have to not only put their toys away but also straighten up their room. The added work will remind your child that there are consequences to lying. Other positive punishment ideas include having your child do something nice for someone they hurt or asking them to finish their homework as soon as they get out of school if they slack off in favor of playing games.

Negative Punishment

Negative punishments involve taking something away in response to bad behavior. This could mean physically taking something from them, like a toy or game; getting rid of privileges, such as TV time or dessert after dinner; or showing them less positive attention until they correct their behavior. You might put your child in time-out if they try to be disruptive to get your attention, or you may refuse to acknowledge a tantrum until they calm down or ask you for help calming down.

It's important to be cautious about what you choose to take away. Ideally, the item or privilege you restrict should be related to what your child did wrong, as this establishes a clear cause and effect. You should never take away something your child needs to fulfill their basic needs, like a nutritious meal or hours of sleep, as this could harm their development and make it harder for them to concentrate on being good.

Positive Reinforcement

Positive reinforcement should be used to encourage kids to repeat good behaviors. It involves giving your child something as a reward for being good. This might be something physical, like a treat or a toy, or simply giving them praise. For example, if you notice your child being kind to someone else on the playground, you might tell them what a good job they did, or offer to take them out for ice cream. Don't forget to reward these behaviors, especially when your child does them before you have to ask. If they do their chores without needing to be reminded, this is a great opportunity to praise them. You may also allow kids to spend more time doing fun things like playing outside, watching TV, or using the computer if their behavior has been especially good.

Positive reinforcement is one of the most effective methods for teaching kids which behaviors are acceptable and which are not. Kids feel great about getting rewarded, while consequences typically make them feel bad and could harm their self-esteem. This doesn't mean you should never punish your child, but you should try to balance these punishments out with rewards so your child can see what awaits them if they can control themselves and act appropriately.

In all cases of behavioral modification, staying consistent is key. Kids need to know what the boundaries are for their behavior and what the results of their actions will be. If you are inconsistent with your punishments and praises, forgetting or purposefully not disciplining them sometimes and levying harsh punishments other times, your child will be confused, and they'll have a harder time following the rules even if they want to. Make sure your child knows what's expected of them and what will happen if they exceed or fail to meet these expectations.

ALTERNATIVES TO PUNISHMENT THAT SUPPORT HIGH SELF-ESTEEM

One significant problem with using punishment to curb aggression is that it often leads to self-esteem issues. Kids begin to see themselves in a more negative light when they notice their parents are frequently angry with them. This can lead them to believe there's something wrong with them, or that they're incapable of acting appropriately, which often leads them to leave their aggression unchecked. They only become angrier with each punishment, and they may feel disconnected from you if they feel like you're being unfair.

Luckily, there are plenty of alternatives to punishment that avoid this unfortunate consequence. You can discipline your child without making them feel like they're fundamentally wrong or that they can never please you. Try these methods of discipline and watch how they allow self-esteem to flourish while still providing reasonable consequences for aggression and defiance.

Prevention

Oftentimes the best way to discourage bad behaviors is to take proactive steps to reduce their likelihood. Many kids have difficulties with impulse control. They may have every intention of leaving the cookies on the counter untouched until after they've eaten dinner, but if they happen to walk by the package and it's within their reach, they may find themselves unable to resist.

You can help kids avoid bad behaviors by making them more difficult to engage in whenever possible. This means putting the cookies on a higher shelf or in a cabinet, where they're not so easily accessible. In other circumstances, this might mean removing your child from a stressful situation before they can get frustrated or keeping a watchful eye on them so they know you'll be there to notice any bad behaviors.

Offer Alternatives

Kids often engage in messy or otherwise unpleasant activities out of pure curiosity or a lack of forethought, often failing to notice the negative consequences of their actions until it is too late. You can offer them possible alternatives that wouldn't cause as much harm. If your child tends to break things when they're angry, provide them with a pillow to hit instead, which can withstand the beating without anyone getting hurt or anything important getting destroyed. If they make a mess in the process of learning something new, have them conduct their experiments outside, or encourage them to use something easier to clean up. These easy alternative tasks eliminate messes and stresses, redirecting attention to a harmless outlet and eliminating the need for punishment of any kind. This can also help kids feel a sense of agency too, as they can continue to do what they wanted, just in another setting or context.

Self-Reflection

Engage in self-reflection whenever possible. While the goal of this book is to help you teach your child about emotional intelligence, this involves learning some emotional intelligence skills yourself from time to time. Self-reflection can make a big difference in how you react to things your child does wrong. Ask yourself questions and check in on yourself to make sure you're not about to explode at your child. If necessary, wait to decide on an appropriate consequence until some of the anger has eased so you can be sure you're choosing something appropriate for the occasion.

Joint Time-Out

Giving kids a time-out is a common punishment. A less common version of this punishment involves giving yourself a time-out as well. This somewhat unusual disciplinary action can actually be surprisingly helpful. When your child acts out, you're likely to be frustrated as well. The time-out gives you both some time to cool off before you say or do something regrettable. It also takes both of you away from the frustrating circumstance or environment, letting you enter a neutral space together. From here, it is much easier to be kind to one another.

Use a Physical Demonstration

We often tell kids to "use your words," but sometimes words aren't as clear as more active forms of communication. If your words don't seem to be getting through to your child, try engaging them physically instead. Ask them to do something, then physically intervene and help them accomplish the task. For example, if your child starts painting and is getting dangerously close to painting on the table, you might ask them to spread out newspapers on the floor or take their supplies outside instead. Once you ask, help them follow your instructions by scooping them up and moving them, trying to make the change more fun by bouncing them or running as you do so. This turns a command into a positive exchange that's more fun for all involved.

Teach Kids to Express Remorse With Actions

Just as you saw in the previous example, actions often speak louder than words. It's one thing to ask your child to apologize after they've done something wrong. Kids may say they're sorry but still feel little remorse over their actions, only offering a half-hearted apology. It's an entirely different situation if you have them prove they're really sorry with their actions.

Observe how your child acts after they do something they shouldn't. Do they take steps to correct their behavior and make it up to you, or are they sullen and silent even after you pry an apology from them? If kids have an active role in their apologies, they'll find they can have a real impact on how well these apologies are received, and that they have an opportunity to repair the situation. Once kids know this, they're more likely to sincerely apologize and undo some of the harm they caused on their own in the future.

Practice Active Listening

Bad behavior may be a result of feeling unheard. If you have a busy household or if your other responsibilities leave you with little time to have genuine conversations with your child, they might act out to try to get your attention. While they're not getting positive attention, they may come to believe this is the only time where your whole focus is on them, which leads them to repeat it again and again. In these cases, you can reduce the likelihood of bad behaviors just by taking some time to listen to them. When your child feels like they're being heard when they're expressing themselves, they usually won't need to engage in more maladaptive behaviors any longer, as they know they have your attention without being destructive or disobedient.

Ask Mundane Questions

If you're looking for a way to help your child calm down after they've become frustrated or upset, try having them answer mundane, unrelated questions. Ask them about things that happened earlier in the day, their likes and dislikes, and similar topics. As your child answers these questions, they'll be distracted from the source of their frustration, and they'll slowly start to let some of that anger go. No longer able to fixate on why they were mad, you'll both be in a better place to assess what happened and decide what should happen next.

Provide an Expectation and Time

When we have our kids apologize or otherwise do things to make up with the person they hurt, it can sometimes come off as less than genuine. After all, we're the ones telling them to apologize, so they might not actually feel sorry for what they did at all, and they may feel like whatever we tell them to do is just another task they have to complete to avoid more punishment. As an alternative to this, let your child know you expect them to show how they're sorry, and then give them the time to do so. This way, your child can regain some of their agency and make the choice to apologize on their own. They'll feel like it was their idea all along, and they'll usually gain more from the experience since they don't think of it as something they were forced to do.

Navigating punishment and other consequences can be tricky when your child has difficulties managing their anger. You don't want to discourage them from reacting completely, but you also don't want to enable their behaviors. By remaining calm yourself, staying consistent, and seeking out methods of discipline that promote greater emotional intelligence rather than functioning purely as a reprimand, you may find that these aggressive tendencies fade away in time.

5

THE ULTIMATE GUIDE TO MINDFULNESS

Mindfulness has become a popular method for dealing with powerful emotions without suppressing them. It can assist in increasing emotional intelligence and improving control over how these emotions are expressed. It may help in minimizing emotional distress, easing the symptoms of depression and other mental health conditions, and dealing with general everyday stressors. While mindfulness is commonly used by adults, it shows great promise as a tool allowing kids to feel more in control of their emotions as well.

The practice of mindfulness is similar to meditation. It involves having a moment of full awareness of where we are and how we're feeling, all without judgment. Under normal circumstances, ruminating endlessly on an unpleasant emotion can leave us in an even worse mood than when we started, often because we feel guilty or ashamed about the power the emotion has over us. However, when we practice mindfulness, we can dissipate this shame and simply see ourselves in a neutral, even kind light. We accept our feelings, ensuring we don't shove them away, and we allow ourselves to feel fully so we can calm ourselves enough to decide how we can best express these feelings in a healthy way.

BENEFITS OF MINDFULNESS

Kids can put mindfulness techniques to use just like adults can. It's a great practice that gives kids a totally safe way to feel more in-tune with their feelings and naturally prevents them from getting frustrated with themselves for feeling upset. It can also be used to help kids fully enjoy the experience of being happy and to assist them in recognizing the things that make them feel calm so they can use this knowledge to relax when under pressure. The benefits of mindfulness are many, and the practice should not be overlooked in any emotional intelligence toolkit.

Less Reactivity

Impulsive behaviors are hard to curb, especially if there is nothing stopping kids from leaping right to their initial reaction. If there is no reason for them to slow down and think, they'll probably jump right to getting upset, letting their emotions get the best of them. When kids routinely practice mindfulness, they get into the habit of slowing down their thoughts and processing things before leaping to conclusions. They give themselves time to consider their reaction to problems and adjust as needed, which reduces the stress of otherwise upsetting incidents.

Suppose your child is sharing their toy with their friend, and their playmate accidentally breaks it. If they're not used to using mindfulness, they might start to cry or get angry with their friend right away. They may accuse them of breaking it on purpose, even if that makes little sense. A child who is well-versed in mindfulness and emotional intelligence, on the other hand, can disregard these initial reactions and come to the conclusion that their friend wasn't trying to break the toy. This can soothe their anger and help them forgive their friend.

Improvements in Emotional Comprehension

By slowing things down, mindfulness helps kids identify how they're feeling at any given moment. If feelings pass by unnoticed, it is harder to see how they impact thoughts and behaviors. When kids pause and think about their emotions, they get more practice naming them and recognizing their effects. They can identify and acknowledge their feelings, which supports healthier coping mechanisms that aren't driven by blind instinct. Kids can also respond to stressful situations with a more open mind and a better understanding of why they feel the way they do.

Greater Emotional Recognition

Because kids learn so much about their own feelings, they also become better at spotting others' emotions. They may see watery eyes and a wobbling lip and be able to tell someone is very sad, because they've felt themselves exhibit the same behaviors when they felt the same way. They can see laughter and smiles and recognize that someone is happy because they've felt the pull of a smile on their own face and they connected the feeling with happiness. The more practice kids get identifying feelings, whether they're their own or someone else's, the easier time they'll have fitting into social situations.

Stronger Control of Emotions

The more kids engage in mindfulness, the better they become at choosing how to handle their feelings. They get used to the simple act of taking a step back and pausing before reacting. This is just enough time for them to take stock of their feelings and discard an initial reaction that seems too excessive. Kids learn to control and govern their emotional expression, and also to decide which emotions help them most for different activities. For example, feelings like positivity and excitement are more helpful at school than despair and guilt. Kids slowly learn to express the best, most appropriate emotions for their situation.

Altogether, practicing mindfulness helps kids and adults alike find their center of balance. Kids feel like they're in the "driver's seat" in regards to their feelings, controlling what they choose to express rather than being controlled by their emotions.

HOW KIDS UTILIZE MINDFULNESS PRACTICES

While people of all ages can use mindfulness to their advantage, it is especially useful for young kids who need some assistance with their emotions. Teaching mindfulness to kids gives them powerful, important tools they can use to navigate difficult times in their lives. They build their confidence and manage their stress levels, and they typically have more success dealing with complicated interpersonal problems.

Treat the cultivation of mindfulness like a habit. The earlier your child adopts a habit, the more likely it is to stick with them for the rest of their lives. Habits like brushing your teeth and showering are small actions we do every day to stay healthy, primarily because our parents showed us how to do them when we were small. Mindfulness is just another helpful habit to add to the pile. By teaching kids mindfulness when they're just starting to monitor their emotions, you give them a head start in emotional intelligence and provide them with a way to process their feelings they can use for many years to come. You also instill the habit of being kind, peaceful, and accepting of themselves and of others.

Since there is so much cognitive development that occurs during the early years of life, mindfulness becomes even more impactful. As kids begin to reason things out and use skills like focus and cognitive control, both of which involve the use of the prefrontal cortex just like mindfulness, they become better at patience, self-regulation, and making judgment calls. These are invaluable skills for any child.

Shaping Critical Skills

Mindfulness has the added benefit of assisting kids in developing three critical skills that are primarily developed during the early childhood years. These skills are information recall, swapping between different tasks, and having appropriate interactions with other people.

The ability to pay attention and retain information is a huge part of early education, as kids spend a large portion of their days in classrooms. Their education is equally benefited by the ability to easily switch their attention back and forth to different areas of focus, as they learn information in a number of different subjects throughout the day. Learning about appropriate behaviors with others helps them socialize effectively and maintain friendships. Other useful benefits provided by mindfulness according to various studies include increased focus, attention, self-control, participation, and compassion; improved academic performance, conflict resolution skills, and overall well-being; and decreased levels of stress, anxiety, depression, and disruptive behaviors (Mindful, n.d., para. 16). With all of these benefits, introducing your child to mindfulness is a no-brainer.

BASIC MINDFULNESS EXERCISES

You conduct a mindfulness exercise similarly to how you would perform a meditation, with the same focus on awareness and breath. The key difference is that in mindfulness, there should be less "clearing your mind" and more consideration of your current place in the world and how you feel. It can be difficult to get kids to sit still long enough for a full mindfulness session, as they often have an abundance of energy and less patience. In this case, you can cut your mindfulness exercise down to a brief few minutes so kids can still work through each stage without giving up before they reach the end.

The three basic practices of mindfulness are mindful breathing, a body scan, and a heartbeat exercise.

Mindful Breathing

Mindful breathing involves finding somewhere comfortable to rest, relaxing your posture, and taking slow, even breaths in through the nose and out through the mouth. You can have your kids follow along with a prerecorded short mindfulness exercise, or you can guide them through it yourself. During this exercise, the goal is to help kids visualize their breath like a living thing that affects the world around them. You might have them imagine they're blowing dandelion petals away in the wind, or that they're softly blowing on a candle, light and steady enough that the flame doesn't go out. As kids keep their breaths slow and steady, their body naturally relaxes and stress melts away.

Body Scan

The body scan is one of the easiest exercises for kids to grasp. Start out by having everyone lay down on their backs and shut their eyes. Next, have them tense and relax different muscles. Start out by having them squeeze all of their muscles, then move through different parts of the body, starting with the feet and working your way up to the shoulders and neck area. This exercise is great as a way to ground kids and help them narrow their thoughts to the present moment, quieting anxieties or regrets. It also allows them to feel more connected to their bodies.

Heartbeat Exercise

In the heartbeat exercise, kids learn how their heart rate can fluctuate as they get more excited, whether this excitement comes from exercise or from their emotional reactions. They get used to noticing the feeling of their heart beating, and are subtly encouraged to consider how stress and anger might also affect the heartbeat. Begin by having kids elevate their heart rate through jogging in place or doing jumping jacks. Then direct their attention to their breath and the feeling of their heart under their fingers so they can detect the increased heart rate. You can then explain how the heart rate picks up in pace with different emotions as well.

BEST PRACTICES FOR MINDFULNESS

As in many other areas of childhood education, the best way to pass on mindfulness skills is to first learn and practice them yourself. You must embody mindfulness in order to pass it along as a good role model for your child. Let your kids see you performing a mindfulness exercise, and if they're interested, invite them to come join you. If not, let them sit quietly with you until you finish, but only if they agree not to disturb you. It's important to let kids feel like they made an active choice to participate, as otherwise, they might quickly grow bored and restless if they feel forced into it.

Try to keep the meditations simple. There are many guided mindfulness exercises available for kids online. If you'd like to use your own, you can start with a brief mantra meditation where you offer compassion and good luck to your loved ones. It may take a while for your child to settle themselves enough to complete their first mindfulness exercise, and a bit longer before you start seeing noticeable results, but in time you'll likely see them become more calm and collected in the face of emotional turmoil.

Tips for Successful Practicing

Mindfulness should be used in positive situations. It is not a punishment, though it can be a way for kids to settle themselves when they feel worried or bothered by something. Don't expect mindfulness to abruptly end bad behaviors, as it's not really equipped to do so; it is merely a way to encourage inner reflection and get kids to feel more in-tune with their feelings.

It can help to turn mindfulness into part of your daily routine. You and your child might like to do it first thing in the morning as a way to prepare yourself for the day ahead, or right after your child gets home from school to relax from the tensions of the day. It could also be a good exercise for relaxation right before bed. Whenever you decide to do it, try to keep it consistent so it becomes a habit.

You can make mindfulness even more effective by preparing a room to feel more calming and inviting. Find somewhere quiet and still where you won't be interrupted. Make sure there aren't any nearby distractions like a TV or toys. You can light some candles so long as you can place them out of kids' reach. If you practice mindfulness routinely, it may be worth setting aside a specific corner of a room as the mindfulness zone so you don't have to prepare the room each time.

Sharing your experiences is another important aspect of mindfulness. Let your child know how the mindfulness exercise makes you feel and what you gain from it. Encourage them to share their own experiences as well. If they don't seem to be getting much out of it, consider adding different exercises that might appeal to them more, and check in with them again later to see if these exercises have a more desirable effect.

MINDFULNESS ACTIVITIES FOR KIDS

There are many different activities you can do with kids to show them how to be more mindful. Some are more traditional meditation practices, while others are closer to fun games with an emotional spin. Here's a small selection of ideas to choose from:

Mindful Walks

Go on a walk with your child, but instead of spending the walk chatting away, turn your gaze to the scenery. Try to notice things you've never seen before, even if you've walked the same path a hundred times. Open your eyes and ears, and help your child enjoy the moment of simply existing among nature.

Listen to the Bell

This is another exercise that involves listening to sounds. You don't need to use a bell if you don't have access to one. You can substitute it for other things that make an extended ringing or chiming noise like wind chimes, dragging your finger along the rim of a glass with some water in it, or a bell sound played from your phone. Have your child close their eyes and focus on the noise, listening hard for it even as it starts to fade away. See how long the sound remains in the air and holds their focus.

Establish a Gratitude Practice

It's easy for kids to get hung up on the things they would like to have in life. Most kids look at new toys and cry if they aren't allowed to get them. Practicing gratitude is a great mindfulness exercise that can take their minds off what they don't have and help them be more thankful for what they do have.

Gratitude practice can be as simple as asking your child to identify one thing every day that they're grateful for. They might choose something they own like a stuffed animal or toy, a feeling or skill they've been working hard on, or even a friend or family member they like spending time with. This can also become a group activity for the whole family to share what they enjoy most over dinner or during a family night.

Mindful Eating

Mindful eating exercises are a staple of mindfulness education. The actions are simple. Select a small piece of food like a raisin or a square of chocolate, and leave it in your mouth. Eat it very slowly, taking a moment to recognize how it feels, how it tastes, what it smells like, and anything else you can notice. This exercise teaches kids not just to be more present in general, but also to pay more attention to their food choices. Mindful eating can help kids curb overeating as well, as it encourages them to enjoy their meals slowly.

Appreciation Practice

Appreciation practice can help kids cope with disappointment and similar emotions. When kids feel like they've been let down, it can be hard to think about all the good things in their lives. During this exercise, ask your child about what caused their disappointed feelings and why they were hurt. Then, help them shift gears. Ask them if there are other good things in their life to balance out the harm, and help them name three things they appreciate instead. This shifts their focus toward gratitude and brings them back to a calm state after getting upset while still acknowledging their feelings.

Mindful Posing

Different poses can cause us to feel differently. The most popular version of this is the "power pose," where striking a confident stance for a minute or more can actually positively impact your confidence levels. There are also mindfulness poses that allow kids to reap the benefits of pride and peacefulness. You can help your child get into the Superman pose, where the feet are planted shoulder-width apart and their arms reach up into the sky, or the Wonder Woman pose, which involves a wider stance and hands on hips.

Spidey-Senses

If your child is a big fan of superheroes, this is the perfect way to frame a mindfulness exercise. Have your child pretend they have spidey-senses and they can notice everything in their nearby environment. Using all five of their senses, have them describe the world around them, paying attention to everything they can see, hear, smell, feel, and taste. This is a unique method for helping kids ground themselves and live in the moment.

The Mindful Jar

The mindful jar is a visualization exercise for strong emotions. Start by nearly filling a clear jar with water, then adding a tablespoon's worth of glitter glue into the jar. Seal the lid tight and give it a shake. The water should appear cloudy and hard to see through with the glitter glue. Explain to your child how the glue represents their negative thoughts, which can cloud their minds and make it hard to think clearly. Next, set the jar back down on the table and let the glue settle. This shows how once they take a step back and relax, the difficult emotions fade and no longer get in the way, so they can better solve their problems with a clear and relaxed mind.

Mindful Breath Exercises

There are many mindfulness breathing exercises in addition to the basic version with steady, measured breaths. A fun one for kids is belly breathing, where kids watch their bellies rise and fall with their breaths. This can help them feel more connected to their bodies as they regulate their breathing speed. A variation on this is teddy bear breathing, where kids repeat the process but this time, they lay down on their backs and rest a stuffed animal on their stomachs. As their belly expands and contracts, the stuffed animal moves up and down along with it.

Apps and Videos

You can use technology to assist in mindful meditation practices. Many apps have video or audio recordings for your child to follow along with. Smiling Minds is a free app that hosts hundreds of meditation guides. It also has instructions for the body scan exercise. Another popular app for kids' meditations is Still Quiet Place, which has animated videos specifically catered toward young kids to keep them engaged.

Exercises for Very Young Kids

Very young kids in preschool and kindergarten may face greater difficulties trying to pay attention for a whole mindfulness exercise. To combat this, you can use very simple, brief exercises to give kids a taste of what mindfulness feels like and expand upon this later.

Try having kids simply notice their breathing and get a feel for what it feels like when they're paying attention. You can also try the five-finger starfish meditation, which involves kids holding out a hand with fingers splayed. As they breathe, have them trace up and down each finger, going up one side on the intake and down the other on the expelled breath. Especially young kids might find it easier to simply count to ten breaths, holding up a finger each time they complete a cycle.

HOW TO BE A MINDFUL FAMILY

Mindfulness isn't just about doing a certain exercise every once in a while. It becomes a part of your family. To be a mindful family is to treat emotions with respect and value, and to make sure every member of the family is comfortable talking about their feelings. It is also to express emotions in safe, healthy ways, and to take a moment to calm down before letting your emotions take control.

Mindful families follow common procedures that fall in line with their values. To become a mindful family, practice the art of embracing imperfection and forgiving people for their momentary mistakes. Listen fully when other family members are talking about their problems, and talk about your emotions without fear of judgment. Appreciation and gratitude should be core components in the household, as should generosity and support. Finally, incorporate play and having fun in daily activities. Mindful families uphold the values of mindfulness, and in doing so, improve the emotional intelligence of the entire household.

WHAT EVERY PARENT OUGHT TO KNOW ABOUT DEALING WITH DIFFICULT SITUATIONS

From time to time, you will have to have difficult conversations with your child. You may need to explain troubles like bullies, death, and even the dangers that linger in the world. These are tough conversations, but they can be made better by practicing emotional honesty. As hard as this may be, helping your child through the emotions that come with these circumstances is part of caring for your child.

ENCOURAGING YOUR CHILD TO OPEN UP TO YOU

When you have to broach a difficult subject with your child, pay attention to possible conversation starters. Look for natural ways to ease into these discussions so kids don't feel like they're being put on the spot. You can help your child relax by starting off with non-judgmental questions that still require serious answers. You might ask them if their friends at school ever mention relationships if you want to talk about boyfriends and girlfriends with them, or who they sat with at lunch today if you suspect there might be a problem within their friend group. These questions will get far more useful answers than general questions like, "How was school?"

Give your child space to talk about their experiences and problems, and don't immediately offer advice or possible solutions. Like adults, kids sometimes just need someone to offer their sympathies, and listening can often help you learn much more about a problem than you'd get trying to solve it right away. Be sure to strike up these kinds of conversations each day, so more serious topics won't be such a significant departure from what they're used to. If you find your child isn't giving you the answers you expected or they seem reluctant to talk, take a step back and revise your approach until they're more at ease with your questions. Avoid getting angry, even if you get a rude or blank rebuff.

Be sure to remain physically engaged and emotionally available throughout the conversation. Let your expressions and gestures do some of the talking for you to avoid interrupting. Above all else, let your child know you're listening to them, and help them work through their emotions as needed.

Preschoolers

Because of their age, you should ask preschoolers more direct, specific questions to encourage them to open up about a subject. Instead of asking about the best part of their day, ask what part of their lunch they liked best, or ask them to choose between two options so they can easily assess their emotions and come to a solution.

If you notice something is off from your observations, ask them about it in a gentle, open way. You might mention how they had a certain expression when you picked them up after school and ask why. If they tell you something happened that made them upset, avoid overreacting. It doesn't help your child to immediately involve you in their affairs if they'd rather handle things on their own. Make sure they're not being harmed, empathize with them and offer your help if needed, and allow the conversation to move on when your child is ready.

Little Kids

Little kids are more comfortable with moments of silence. You may feel closer to your child when you simply spend time together, whether you're speaking or not. This can be a good exercise at the end of the day when you're both letting the stresses of work and school slide off your backs. Moments like bedtime tuck-ins and car rides are great opportunities for low-pressure chats. It's also a good idea to make sure your day includes some parent-child bonding time. You might sit down together to play a game, work on a puzzle, or help them with homework, but whatever you choose make sure you are strengthening your bond by spending time together.

Big Kids

Once again, car rides provide an excellent opportunity for a conversation with low stakes. Take advantage of this time and other moments of stillness to talk, and remain neutral when your child opens up to you, only interjecting if they ask for a response. Otherwise, allow them to vent some of their frustrations and largely work out a solution to their issues by themselves. If you're talking face-to-face, pay attention to body language, which can often reveal more than their words. While you don't need to make a point to bond with older kids every day, it's still a good idea to schedule something at least once a month.

Handling Avoidant Behavior

You may encounter times where your child reacts strangely to your questions and you start to suspect something is wrong. One common trouble is kids clamming up instead of sharing their feelings and experiences with you. If you believe they're being quiet because they're hiding something from you, consider what might make them act avoidantly or lie. They may feel embarrassed, or they may be doing something they know they shouldn't. The best thing you can do isn't to push them until they admit what they're hiding. Instead, give them the opportunity to come talk to you when they're ready, and remind them you'll care about them no matter what they may be hiding.

If you do feel the need to confront your child, speak plainly and directly without trying to catch them in a lie. Explain that you want to know the truth because you're worried about what might actually be happening. Avoid getting angry when they finally open up, even if the truth is worse than you pictured. This only teaches your child not to be honest with you in the future and that they would have been better off keeping the secret.

If your child simply seems reluctant to talk because they're tired, let them cool down first before you ask about their day. You can tell them, "I'd love to hear what happened today whenever you're ready," so they know you're happy to wait and open to hearing about it at any time. Once they feel like talking, ask specific questions. Keep an eye out for signs that your child might want to talk to you without knowing how to bring something up, like following you around or asking to do an activity together, and make sure to give them your attention during these times.

COMMUNICATING DURING DIFFICULT SITUATIONS

There will come a point where you need to broach a truly difficult subject with your child when they begin facing adversity in their lives. Don't freak out. Help your child develop confidence by remaining calm yourself during these discussions, and let them lead the way in coming up with a solution unless they outright ask you for advice. These discussions can be a great opportunity to reinforce family and community values of support and kindness. To give your child the support they need, make sure you have a good grasp on your own feelings first. Keep an eye out for common signs of distress like a lack of interest or withdrawal, low energy, fear of certain activities, or unusually unruly behaviors. Treat any questions with respect, and never ignore your child when they're trying to talk to you about serious matters. Let kids know they're safe with you, and remember that it's okay to honestly say you don't know how to answer a question yet and that you'll make a plan to find out. Be sure not to add more fear, and don't encourage kids to see their situation as hopeless. You can make these conversations easier by bringing these kinds of topics up regularly so you'll be more prepared when they become an issue for your child.

DEALING WITH TRAUMATIC NEWS OR EVENTS

If you need to convey traumatic news to your child or to help them come to terms with their feelings about the news, it's important to deal with your own feelings first. You can be honest about things like sadness and grief, but don't let them overtake your ability to parent. Keep an eye on their emotional state as well, and look out for nonverbal cues.

Open-ended questions and conversations can help you learn more about the current situation. Ask about how they're feeling, and try to get a sense of exactly what your child knows and understands about the situation. You can skip giving them extra details that aren't necessary for explaining the situation, as these may only confuse and further upset them. Allow yourself to be sympathetic toward any reactions they may have and don't pass judgment on their feelings. Instead, allow them to feel accepted and reassured. Don't avoid or dismiss the subject either, as this could encourage kids not to talk about their problems at all.

There are plenty of difficult or traumatic things kids can encounter during their childhoods. A death in the family, bullying, divorce, and child abuse are just a few of these problems that require more serious discussions, but if you follow this general guidance, you should be able to have an open and honest talk with your child regardless of the topic.

HANDLING THE DEATH OF A LOVED ONE

If at all possible, discussions of death should begin before a loved one passes away. Introduce the topic when someone is injured or ill and prepare them for the possibility that a loved one may not be around anymore. If they are very young, you may need to explain what death means. You can help your child make hospital visits, phone calls, and cards to send to the person who is ill, but don't force them to come along if they aren't comfortable doing so.

After a death occurs, let your child know right away. Again, don't demand their presence at the funeral, but if they'd like to come, let them know what they can expect to see. Make sure your child knows they're secure and safe, even if you're upset by the loss. Be upfront and direct with your language; saying someone died is clearer and often easier for kids to process than saying they passed on or that they've "gone away." Let your child guide the conversation when they're ready, and listen to them if they have concerns. If your child was close with the person who passed away, help them engage in activities to remember them by, like looking at old photos or making a symbolic craft together.

It's possible that your child may worry that you will die too now that they have been introduced to the idea. If this is a concern for them, reassure them by saying something like, "I don't plan on leaving you anytime soon." At the same time, you should also provide reassurance about what would happen to them if you did die, reminding them that other family members would take care of them and help them feel safe again.

BULLYING

Keep an eye out for common signs that your child may be the victim of bullying. They may lose their enthusiasm for school, to the point of developing anxiety about going in the morning. They may be less likely to talk about fun experiences with friends, and they may complain of a stomach ache from their worries. Try to involve yourself in your child's social life through conversations, just so you know who they're spending time with and who they aren't getting along with.

If your child is at a loss about what to do, creating a toolkit for them can provide them with ideas for handling the bully. Here are a few possibilities:

- Help kids come up with phrases to use as firm but non-aggressive responses to the bully, such as, "I didn't like that," and, "leave me alone."
- Engage in role playing scenarios where you pretend to be the bully and you coach your child through their responses.
- Maintain communication with your child about the issue.
- Teach your child how to use confident body language and poses to their advantage.
- Build your child's confidence through extra-curricular activities and family bonding moments so the bullying is less likely to harm their self-esteem.
- Tell your child you're proud of them for standing

up to their bullies no matter what method they choose. Let them know you have their back.

Teach Kids the Right Ways to React

Certain behaviors can actually encourage bullying to continue, while others are effective methods for standing up to bullies. Ensure your child knows a bully can never make them feel bad if they don't allow them to affect their confidence. Encourage your child to tell the bully how they feel and ask them to stop without aggression, as this can lead to a physical fight. Have them avoid rewarding the bully's efforts with tears or other emotional blow-ups, but don't let them go into school every day accepting that they're going to be mistreated. Help your child trust in their instincts and take the path that feels right for them, and take actions of your own to help the situation.

Take Action as a Parent

As a parent, you won't be able to directly stop the bullying unless it happens in front of you. Still, you have more power over the situation by virtue of being an adult. With your child's permission, you can step in and provide support by alerting the teacher and school to the bullying problem, involving the bully's parents, teaching your child good coping skills for getting their emotions in check when they're being antagonized, and encouraging your child to stand up for other kids they see getting bullied.

DIVORCE

Some parents try to wait as long as possible before letting their kids know they're getting a divorce, but this only increases the chances they'll hear it from someone else first. Talk about it with them as soon as possible, and ideally together with their other parent so you can reassure them you'll both remain in their lives. Try to choose a day with plenty of free time, like a weekend, so your child can process their feelings without any rush. Regardless of the real details, try to use a narrative free from explicit blame, as getting angry at your ex-spouse may only upset your child. Still, it's important to give them a general idea of why you two are separating. You can say something like, "We're just not in love anymore, but we both still love you very much." This comforts them while still being as honest as possible without causing distress.

Let your child know what kinds of changes they can expect and what will stay the same. If one of you is leaving the house, let them know before it happens. Let them ask any questions they need to, and allow them time to react in whatever way they see fit without taking it personally. Some kids may be hurt, and some may believe it's their own fault.

Work to consistently reassure them that they did not cause the divorce and they shouldn't blame themselves. Let them adjust to the news before you start to settle into old routines again, as they may become more upset if you try to carry on like nothing is happening. Emotional honesty and openness is key.

CHILD ABUSE

Each situation of child abuse is different, and it should be handled with care. Some kids may appreciate keeping routines as normal as possible while still working to protect them, while others may have trouble going near areas they associate with their abuse. If necessary and if your child is comfortable with it, speak to a child therapist or involve the authorities, but let your child make the decision. Helping them feel a sense of agency is incredibly important.

It can be hard to find the right words to talk about this topic with your child. If you suspect your child might be the victim of abuse, avoid being accusatory, and don't make promises you cannot keep. For example, don't tell your child you promise not to tell anyone, as you may need to in order to guarantee their safety. Instead, tell them you promise to do what you can to help them, and that you won't tell anyone who doesn't need to know. Instead of asking directly if someone touched them inappropriately, you can ask if there's something bothering them and allow them to lead the conversation.

Your child may have questions of their own when discussing the topic of abuse or talking about their experiences. Here are some common questions and possible answers:

- **What is child abuse?**: Child abuse involves an adult purposefully hurting a child. It can be physical, emotional, neglectful, or sexual.
- **Is it my fault if it happens to me?**: Child abuse is never the child's fault. Reassure the child that it is always the fault of the adult, no matter what actions they may have taken.
- **How can I make it stop?**: Many child abusers tell kids they'll be in trouble if they tell someone what's happening, but this is just a way to threaten them. The best way for a child to escape an abusive situation is to tell a trusted adult and allow them to help.

7

THE NINJA GUIDE TO BUILD RESILIENCE IN YOUR CHILD

It may be hard to picture if your child is still young, but there will come a time in their lives where you are no longer constantly around to help them, and they will need to start handling their emotions on their own. They may start to draw away from you and establish their independence as they become teenagers, or this distance may only start to appear when they move away to college or move out of the house as an adult. At a certain point, all kids learn to lead their own lives. There will be times even while they are young, such as when they are at school or a club meeting, that you won't be around to protect them either, and they will need to learn emotional resilience to deal with difficulties and stress from different sources in their lives.

Your ultimate goal as an emotional intelligence educator is to help kids cultivate their emotional skills so they can cope with their feelings by themselves. Emotional resilience represents their ability to handle the different ups and downs they'll experience in their lives, as well as moments of great change. Resilience helps kids find their footing in unfamiliar circumstances and allows them to withstand more significant shake-ups like the end of a relationship, moving, or experiencing grief. It becomes a large part of mental health management as kids get older and enter adulthood. It's important for kids to start building resilience as soon as possible so they can withstand these tough times and much more.

There will be obstacles and setbacks in your child's life, no matter how much you may want to prevent these as a parent. While you can't clear your child's path entirely, you can give them the tools necessary for them to overcome these difficulties so they can avoid stress and anxiety. In fact, dealing with these setbacks can help kids gain experience with emotional intelligence if they have a difficult time learning in more traditional ways. They may strengthen their self-awareness and self-advocacy abilities, boost their self-esteem, and expose them to different strategies for emotional regulation and self-improvement. In this way, while these obstacles aren't necessarily a good thing, they help to build character and support healthy development.

HOW TO HELP YOUR CHILD CULTIVATE RESILIENCE

Resilience is a skill that can come from many different sources. It can be a natural product of experiencing a difficult moment in life and making it through to the other side. Kids can develop resilience by relying on support from their families, friends, and community members, as they never truly face adversity alone. And of course, parents play a major role in helping their kids develop resilience. Each of these methods can be useful and impart different lessons to your child.

Parents and Other Adults

It's very likely that you've experienced some form of hardship during your life. Maybe you struggled to fit in as a child. Perhaps you had some financial troubles that made you worry about your ability to afford everything you needed to live safely and happily. You may have experienced a significant loss and the grief that comes along with it. Whatever your life experiences, you know what it is to experience pain and hurt, and to make it through this hurt to reach a supportive, loving environment once again. Therefore, you are the best possible role model for resilience for your child. You are living proof that the difficulties you face do not have to define you. When your child sees how calm and collected you are in the face of things that frighten them, they'll become a little braver in turn.

You can also support resilience by teaching your child necessary problem-solving skills. Kids who learn to tackle problems, first with your support and then on their own, are better at recovering from unfortunate events. They are often able to find a suitable solution for their problems, and if not, they are strong enough to hold out until the rough seas of life have calmed down, all because they learned their resilience from you.

Social Support

Kids have an easier time exhibiting resilient behaviors when they know they have a loving, dedicated social circle to back them up. Kids need to feel supported, as do adults. Without social support, it would be very difficult for kids to tackle problems head-on or take risks. With the encouragement and backing of their families, their communities, and their friends, they are emboldened to take on even the toughest of tasks.

Moderately Stressful Situations

A small amount of stress may be difficult in the moment, but it helps kids get a sense of the difficult moments that may await them later in life. Therefore, some stress can be good, so long as it does not become overwhelming. Kids will be expected to push themselves a little harder, and they may find that their limits are much further than they expected them to be. These semi-stressful situations set kids up with skills they'll continue to rely on for much of their lives.

PRACTICAL, POWERFUL STRATEGIES FOR BUILDING RESILIENCE IN KIDS

Kids can benefit greatly from getting some resilience practice in. A small stressful situation may help them feel a little more comfortable with the idea of testing their limits, but they may face much more significant disappointments in their lives. Because of this, it's important to take every possible opportunity to educate kids on resilience so they'll have it when they need it most.

Help Kids Build Social Connections

There is very little that's more comforting for kids than having a good support group. Always work to increase the amount of time your child spends around people who support them. It's very likely that at some point, they will come across people who don't want to see them succeed. You can counteract this by repeatedly and frequently showing your child that there will always be people who are supportive of their dreams and goals. Let them know it's always okay to ask for help when they need it. This knowledge will provide them with strength in their most hopeless times.

Support Their Executive Functioning Skills

Executive functioning involves important skills including self-control, critical thinking, and working memory. These kinds of skills are significantly helpful for resilience, as they are all part of problem-solving and emotional management. Some behaviors involved in executive functioning include healthy social behavior, as modeled by you; establishing consistent routines; creating and maintaining supportive relationships; providing opportunities for social connections completely unique to your child, such as friendships outside the family and romantic relationships; games that involve memory and engage kids' creative thinking skills; and chances to think and act independently based on your child's own decisions. You can practice each of these behaviors with your child on a regular basis.

Incorporate Exercise

Many people use exercise as a way to channel their emotions into positive energy. Some have used it as a method for expressing their grief in a constructive way, while others have used workouts to cope with a serious life event like a new job or a breakup. Staying active helps kids remain healthy, and it serves as a great outlet for lots of pent up energy your child may be carrying around. On top of that, it's an excellent healthy habit for adults to practice, and the best way to convince yourself to exercise later in life is to practice it religiously as a child.

Nurture Feelings of Competency and Optimism

When we get discouraged or disappointed, we tend to forget just how much we are truly capable of. Sometimes we need to be reminded of everything we do well. Don't forget to let your child know what they excel in and how proud you are of them trying their best, no matter how their results pan out. Praise your child for the effort they put into their tasks, and reassure them that even if it doesn't seem like they're the best suited for a task at first, they can always try to improve. With enough dedication and practice, they're sure to succeed, regardless of what they're up against.

Help Kids Reframe Challenges and Face Fears

Some challenging or frightening situations can appear scarier at first glance than they actually are. For example, your child may stress out about an upcoming math test, worried they're not going to do well and their grades will suffer. To counteract this, you can point out that this math test is just one part of a larger grade, and even if they don't do as well as they hope, there are other ways to keep their grades up. You may also remind them that grades aren't everything, but if they want some help studying, you would be happy to assist them. By providing your support and reducing the threat of the challenge, you take away some of its power and remind your child that they are capable of handling almost anything.

Let Kids See How You Handle Disappointment

Many parents are afraid to show their negative emotions around their kids. They remain somewhat distant and withdrawn, which can leave kids wondering why they never see their parents struggling the same way they do. Rather than helping your child grow, this practice only leaves them seeing themselves as lesser or deficient. It can help to let your child see how you handle a wide range of emotions, especially disappointment. Be honest with them and explain that while you're not happy with what happened, you know that there will be another opportunity for something good to happen later, and that you'll make it through this tough moment if you stick to your healthy coping strategies. By seeing that their parent is just as capable of getting disappointed as they are, but also that this feeling can be managed, your child will likely be inspired to face their own disappointments with the same level of resilience.

Encourage Relatively Safe, Considered Risks

Sometimes, it's necessary to encourage kids to take risks and see how things pan out for themselves. This doesn't mean you should let them experience a complete trial by fire, but it does mean that if you find yourself acting like a helicopter parent from time to time, you should try taking a step back and letting them make some mildly risky decisions. Experience is the best way for them to learn, after all. If they never try to take risks in their childhood, they'll have trouble taking advantage of opportunities later in life.

Let Kids Experience Consequences and Lessons

Risks may not always pan out, and bad decisions come with consequences. When this happens, it's tempting to want to sweep your child up and protect them from any possible harms that could befall them. However, this just isn't a realistic method of parenting. Sometimes, it is necessary to let your child lie in the bed they've made so they can learn from the experience. If they fail a test because they spent the night watching TV instead of studying, let them deal with the failing grade. Next time, they won't be so quick to brush off their responsibilities.

Give Kids Some Agency

This is another resilience-building strategy that encourages letting kids make their own choices. When they're very young, you can start by offering them small, less significant choices and allowing them to decide what they want. For example, you could ask them what side they want with their lunch out of three different options. As they get older, you can let them make more important choices, while still being around to offer advice and support them should they need it. Letting kids experience a little agency helps them feel more in control of their lives. It also reduces the chances of them making unsafe decisions when they move out or go to college, as it won't be the first time they've felt like they were in charge of themselves.

Nurture a Growth Mindset

Many kids feel more limited when they feel like they are only good at certain subjects. They make the mistake of believing they aren't capable of getting better at the things they don't immediately excel at, which discourages them from trying new things. This is in stark opposition to the growth mindset, which suggests that with enough practice and attention, people can learn any skill they want. A growth mindset is healthier and helps kids be more productive, as they don't box themselves into certain assumptions about who they are and what kind of person they can be. Kids with growth mindsets aren't nearly as negatively impacted by failure, as they know they can always try again and they might have more favorable results next time. This helps them remain resilient even when things aren't going their way.

Help Kids Create a Problem-Solving Toolbox

Plenty of parents try to solve their kids' problems for them. They interject themselves into every issue, often calling the school or other kids' parents, frequently getting involved without their kids asking them to. While it's good to have your child's back through thick and thin, there will come a time when they need to stand on their own two legs without backing down. If you've been intervening too frequently, your child might not have the experience they need to deal with problems by themselves.

Rather than directly interfering, try creating a problem-solving toolbox for your child. The problem-solving toolbox contains different strategies for conflict resolution, emotional control, stress management, and other necessary activities that could otherwise be hard for kids to tackle alone. Encourage your child to develop their own strategies for dealing with personal and academic issues, and they will naturally add these strategies to their toolbox for future use.

Use Delayed Gratification

Instant gratification is a deceptively dangerous habit for kids to indulge in. It represents the idea that the immediate pleasure that can be gained from an activity is more desirable than long-term results. Indulging in instant gratification means giving up a better reward for something easier. An example of instant gratification might be your child choosing not to do their homework in favor of playing with their friends. In the moment, it is much more fun to play with friends than it is to read a textbook. However, the next day when their homework is incomplete for class, they may regret giving into instant gratification.

Delayed gratification, on the other hand, encourages kids to hold out for the better long-term reward. Maintaining good grades is much more valuable than a few extra minutes at the playground, so the homework should be prioritized. This can often be difficult for kids to understand, as they are impulsive and want the easy prize without the extra work. You can help your child understand the value of delayed gratification by asking them to weigh the value of two things in their head, one a short-term pleasure and the other a long-term achievement, and think about how they'd feel if they had each one. The long-term achievement holds more weight, so kids will eventually start to see the value in holding out for the better prize. As a simple example, ask them to choose between getting one piece of candy now, or behaving themselves while you run errands and getting two pieces after. The two pieces of candy should win out, which means your child not only learns about long-term goal setting but also practices their good behavior skills.

Delayed gratification ties into self-control and self-discipline, which are key factors in remaining resilient. If kids remember that there is something better waiting for them at the end of every one of life's difficulties, they will be able to withstand these difficult situations without issue.

Avoid Sink or Swim Situations

Kids learn best when they can try out some things for themselves, but they must also know they are supported and loved. They want to branch out and explore the world, but they also want to know they have a home base to come back to. Let your child try new things and put themselves out there while reminding them you are here for them should they need it. This will provide them with the confidence they need to tackle their new passion head-on.

Your child may also benefit from learning to ask for help more frequently. Encourage them to talk to teachers when they don't understand a new concept, or to ask their fellow students for help. You can also use the scaffolding approach to providing support, which involves offering a lot of support at the beginning of the exercise and slowly walking it back, letting your child take the reins as time goes on. This is similar to how you might teach them to ride a bike, starting off with training wheels and steadying hands, and eventually letting them ride on their own.

ACTIVITIES FOR TEACHING GRIT AND RESILIENCE

Resilience can also be taught through encouragement and trying out various activities. Practice them with your child to help them refine their emotional management skills. You'll also help your child develop grit, which is a mixture of passion and perseverance.

Assist Kids in Identifying Their Goals

Everyone needs something to work toward in their lives. The pursuit of goals is at the top of Maslow's hierarchy of needs. It represents a feeling of self-fulfillment we get from feeling like we've found our place in the world. You can help your child achieve this same feeling by walking them through the process of creating goals for themselves. You can assist them in creating a mood board, or even just daydreaming and journaling about their goals. Consider both short-term goals that can be accomplished now and long-term goals they can strive for their whole lives.

Encourage Your Child to Talk to People With Admirable Goals

Kids naturally look up to their parents, but there are plenty of other people who might be good role models for your child as well. Consider people you can get in contact with who have goals similar to your child's ambitions, or who have especially altruistic goals, and who work toward those goals each day. Show kids that hard work and perseverance really does pay off and that their dreams are entirely achievable if they believe in themselves and they're willing to work for them.

Use Nature and Literature

There are plenty of examples of grit and resilience to be found in the world around us. You only need to look outside to see them. Show your child how grass or flowers might push through the cracks in the sidewalks to grow in inhospitable conditions, which shows a remarkable amount of resilience, or let them watch documentaries about animals that live in harsh environments or otherwise demonstrate the value of hard work. You can also look to books for these inspirational stories. One especially well-known children's story is *The Little Engine That Could*, which is all about the power of persistence and positive thinking.

Ask Kids What the Hard Part Is

When your child seems discouraged and they're ready to give up on their task, help them find the will to keep going by asking them, "What's the hard part?" When they answer, help them break this difficult roadblock into smaller, more manageable pieces by gently guiding them toward a more incremental approach. Let your child figure this new approach out themselves so they get the experience of flexing their problem-solving skills.

As an example, let's say your child is trying to complete a drawing and they're having difficulties. When you ask what the hard part is, they say they can't get the tree to look right. They can then break the process of drawing the tree down into its smaller parts—an evergreen tree is little more than a small brown rectangle for a trunk and a big green triangle for the branches. Thinking about hard tasks in terms of their smallest, simplest components breaks down barriers to success and teaches kids to tackle other problems in much the same way.

Follow the "Hard Thing" Rule

The "hard thing" rule is a study in dedication broken into three rules. The first rule is that everyone in the family has to pick something hard to focus their efforts on for a while. Usually the time period is around a month minimum. The task should be difficult enough that it requires multiple attempts and some trial-and-error to get right. The second rule is that everyone gets to choose their own hard task. The third rule is that whatever you choose to start, you have to finish. This encourages kids to pick up new skills, try out new experiences, and broaden their horizons, all while having them stick with it long enough that they can see their hard work pay off.

Grit Pie Exercise

The "grit pie" activity is meant to help kids practice optimism. The pie is symbolic of a larger obstacle your child is facing, while each slice of the pie functions as a 'slice' of the problem. For example, the whole pie might be doing well in math class, and the slices may include problems such as the teacher moving too fast or your child failing to turn in their homework. Decide together if each part of the issue is a permanent obstacle or if it's something temporary that will go away soon. When the issue is broken down this way, your child will discover that very few issues have permanent reasons why they're problems after all, and that the vast majority of the slices are usually temporary troubles they can easily overcome. A teacher moving too fast might become more manageable with additional math tutoring, and ensuring your child finishes their homework first thing after school ensures they get the practice they need to really learn the lessons. What was once a significant issue is easily solved through divide and conquer.

Share Your Passions

Kids enjoy being able to share fun activities and quality time with their parents, and getting your child involved in your favorite hobby can be a great way to bond. Show your child how excited the hobby makes you and how it's okay to show enthusiasm for what they love. By sharing your passions, you also teach your child that they can pursue their dreams and goals, finding hobbies and even a career they love rather than settling for a job they don't particularly enjoy. This helps your child feel truly limitless.

Leave a 1-Click Review!

I hope you are enjoying my book ! I would be incredibly thankful if you could take just 60 seconds to write a brief review on Amazon, even if it's just a few sentences!

>> Click here or scan the QR Code to leave a quick review

CONCLUSION

At this point, it should be incredibly clear to you just how important emotional intelligence is. EQ is a foundational skill upon which many others are built later in childhood development, including socialization, critical thinking, problem-solving, showing compassion, and much more. Kids who are adequately emotionally prepared tend to experience greater success in their personal relationships, academic careers, and later professional lives. Though the benefits of emotional intelligence remain significant throughout our whole lives, education about feelings is most effective when it starts in early childhood.

As a parent, teacher, or other guardian, you serve as your child's introduction to emotional intelligence. You are both the model upon which they will base themselves and the instruction manual for navigating their various, often confusing feelings. You also provide feedback about how well your child is managing their emotions. You can guide them toward a healthy relationship with their feelings where they appropriately express how they feel and respectfully engage with others.

It is never too early to start teaching kids about their feelings. The more fluent your child is in emotional literacy, the fewer problems they'll face because of a failure to read the room or an unintentionally upsetting behavior. They'll be able to form strong bonds with their peers with the potential to last a lifetime. Emotionally intelligent kids are typically well-liked at their workplaces, and they often have an academic advantage as well, since they are more motivated and driven. In short, there is very little a truly emotionally intelligent child cannot do because they have the self-confidence to put their best efforts into any task and the self-awareness to take care of themselves and others.

In *Raising Emotional Intelligence in Kids*, you've learned how to avoid many of the common pitfalls preventing many parents from providing their kids with adequate emotional awareness. You should now understand why proper emotional development is so critical to your child's future, as well as what steps you can take to encourage their success, whether you're helping your toddler put a name to their emotions or assisting your tween's navigation through the

CONCLUSION | 327

emotional storm that is puberty. Whatever emotional challenges come your family's way, you know you're more than prepared to face the challenge. You're ready to give your child all the tools they need to embrace the world and conquer life.

If you enjoyed this book and found it to be especially helpful, consider leaving a positive review on Amazon. This helps other parents and educators provide their kids with the benefits of emotional intelligence, breaking down barriers to socialization and creating a more compassionate and empathetic world.

REFERENCES

AnnaliseArt. (2020, Mar. 24). *Exercise equipment.* Pixabay. https://pixabay.com/illustrations/workout-equipment-weights-4963665/

AnnaliseArt. (2020, Apr. 16). *Happy face emojis.* Pixabay. https://pixabay.com/illustrations/happy-faces-emoticons-smiley-emoji-5049095/

CASEL. (n.d.). *Approaches.* https://casel.org/what-is-sel-4/approaches/

CASEL. (n.d.). *What are the core competence areas and where are they promoted?* https://casel.org/sel-framework/

Committee for Children. (n.d.). *What is social-emotional learning?* https://www.cfchildren.org/what-is-social-emotional-learning/

CorrelateStudio. (2019, May 8). *Four pairs of friends*. Pixabay. https://pixabay.com/illustrations/friends-people-friendship-family-4187953/

Creozavr. (2019, Dec. 2). *Bullying*. Pixabay. https://pixabay.com/vectors/boy-girl-protection-stood-up-fight-4665536/

DavidRockDesign. (2018, Apr. 17). *Child reading*. Pixabay. https://pixabay.com/illustrations/child-i-am-a-student-book-figure-3326960/

Kadane, L. (2020, Aug. 4). *EQ vs. IQ: Why emotional intelligence will take your kid further in life*. Today's Parent. https://www.todaysparent.com/kids/kids-health/eq-vs-iq-why-emotional-intelligence-will-take-kids-farther-in-life/

Lisitsa, E. (2012, June 8). *An introduction to emotion coaching*. The Gottman Institute. https://www.gottman.com/blog/an-introduction-to-emotion-coaching/

McLeod, S. (2020, Mar. 20). *Maslow's hierarchy of needs*. Simply Psychology. https://www.simplypsychology.org/maslow.html

Mindful. (n.d.). *Mindfulness for kids*. https://www.mindful.org/mindfulness-for-kids/

Mohammad_hassan. (2020, Aug. 21). *Handing over a heart*. Pixabay. https://pixabay.com/illustrations/giving-love-apologize-kind-man-5503676/

Mohammad_hassan. (2017, Aug. 19). *Woman lifting baby into the air*. Pixabay. https://pixabay.com/illustrations/family-mother-child-adult-baby-2658143/

Morin, A. (2019, Oct. 21). *How to raise an emotionally intelligent child*. Verywell family. https://www.verywellfamily.com/tips-for-raising-an-emotionally-intelligent-child-4157946

Ohio University. (n.d.). *5 qualities of emotional intelligence*. https://onlinemasters.ohio.edu/blog/5-qualities-of-emotional-intelligence/

OpenClipart-Vectors. (2017, Jan. 31). *Superman power pose*. Pixabay. https://pixabay.com/vectors/cartoon-comic-comic-characters-2025820/

Oswalt, A. (n.d.). *Emotional and social development in early childhood*. Gracepoint. https://www.gracepointwellness.org/474-emotional-intelligence/article/16149-emotional-and-social-development-in-early-childhood

Piyapong89. (2020, Oct. 22). *Children displaying emotions*. Pixabay. https://pixabay.com/illustrations/children-childhood-young-kids-boys-5672087

RoadLight. (2020, Oct. 9). *Rabbit and fox*. Pixabay. https://pixabay.com/illustrations/animals-cute-animals-wild-animals-5636909/

Syaibatulhamdi. (2020, Feb. 11). *Walk at sunset*. Pixabay. https://pixabay.com/illustrations/wallpaper-cartoon-landscape-people-4839630

Tominey, S., O'Bryon, E., Rivers, S. E., & Shapses, S. (2017, March). *Teaching emotional intelligence in early childhood*. NAEYC. https://www.naeyc.org/resources/pubs/yc/mar2017/teaching-emotional-intelligence

Trezise, K. (2017, July 13). *Emotions in classrooms: The need to understand how emotions affect learning and education.* NJP Science of Learning. https://npjscilearncommunity.nature.com/posts/18507-emotions-in-classrooms-the-need-to-understand-how-emotions-affect-learning-and-education

Trotta, J. (2018, Dec. 10). *Emotional intelligence—What do the numbers mean?* LinkedIn. https://www.linkedin.com/pulse/emotional-intelligence-what-do-numbers-mean-joanne-trotta

Wixin_56k. (2019, May 7). *Bedroom at night*. Pixabay. https://pixabay.com/illustrations/bed-sleep-night-sleeping-4183710/

www.ingramcontent.com/pod-product-compliance
Lightning Source LLC
Chambersburg PA
CBHW061203070526
44579CB00010B/113